Feel the Fear and Do It Anyway

Susan Jeffers

Vermilion
LONDON

16

Published in 2007 by Vermilion, an imprint of Ebury Publishing
Ebury Publishing is a Random House Group company

First published by Century in 1987

The Random House Group Limited Reg. No. 954009

Addresses for companies within the Random House Group can be found at
www.randomhouse.co.uk

A CIP catalogue record for this book is available from the British Library

The Random House Group Limited supports The Forest Stewardship Council®
(FSC®), the leading international forest-certification organisation. Our books
carrying the FSC label are printed on FSC®-certified paper. FSC is the only
forest-certification scheme supported by the leading environmental organisations,
including Greenpeace. Our paper procurement policy can be found at
www.randomhouse.co.uk/environment

Printed and bound by CPI Group (UK) Ltd, Croydon, CR0 4YY

ISBN 978-0-09-190707-5

Copies are available at special rates for bulk orders.
Contact the sales development team on 020 7840 8487 for more information.

To buy books by your favourite authors and register for offers, visit
www.randomhouse.co.uk

Feel the Fear and Do it Anyway®
is a registered trademark

For the wonderful gifts of life and love,
I dedicate this book to the loving memory
of my mother, Jeanne, and my father, Leon.

I also dedicate this book to my jewel of a
husband, Mark Shelmerdine, who brings
so much love and joy into my life.
I am truly blessed.

Contents

Acknowledgments

Everybody needs a cheering squad rooting them on, and my cheerleaders are sensational! *Judith Kendra,* the Publishing Director of Rider, Random House UK who made this 20th Anniversary Edition happen and the many people at Random House who support my efforts; *Martha Lawrence,* whose faith in and appreciation of my work made the original edition *finally* happen 20 years ago; *Dominick Abel,* my agent in the US and *David Grossman,* my agent in the UK, who believed in my work, never gave up and ultimately succeeded; *Ruth Van Doren* and the students at the New School for Social Research in New York City, who gave me a receptive environment to begin teaching my ideas about fear; *Kathryn Welds,* at the UCLA Extension, who welcomed my work in California; *Diana von Welanetz Wentworth,* the late *Paul von Welanetz* and members of The Inside Edge, who stood on chairs and cheered every success; *Roslyn Hayes,* my teacher who many years ago encouraged me to stretch as far as I could go; *Sally Lefkowitz,* an inspiration, who showed me what indomitable courage looks like; *the men and women from around the world* who have let me know that my work has made a difference in their lives . . . you have clearly made a difference in mine; *my loyal and caring friends,* who applaud every step I take . . . I treasure your support; my wonderful sister, *Marcia Jeffers,* who is also my best friend, and my brother-in-law, *Bruce Rabiner,* who does so much to help this world; my fabulous children, *Gerry Gershman* and *Leslie Wandmacher,* and stepchildren, *Alice* and *Guy Shelmerdine,* and their mates, *Michael Wandmacher, Anthony Shelmerdine and Ashley Jacobs;* and, of course, my incredible husband, *Mark Shelmerdine,* who walks beside me and comforts and supports me every step of the way. I thank all of the above for all that you do to bring so much richness into my life . . . Thank you! Thank you! Thank you!

FEEL
THE
FEAR
AND
DO IT
ANYWAY

I do believe in miracles . . . and the success of *Feel the Fear and Do It Anyway* is a miracle to me. So many publishers rejected it in the beginning that I almost gave up trying to have it published. After all, if you received a rejection letter, as I did, that said, "Lady Di could be cycling nude down the street giving this book away, nobody would read it," wouldn't you be tempted to give up trying?!

I actually did put the manuscript away in a drawer for a few years, and almost forgot about it. One day, I decided to clean out that particular drawer . . . and there it was . . . waiting for me. I sat down and read through it again. Suddenly I was struck with the powerful sense that I held something in my hands that would be of help to many people. This time I made a vow to myself: "Somehow I am going to find a way to get *Feel the Fear and Do It Anyway* out into the world!"

And so I "felt the fear" and tried once again to find a publisher. And this time, with a deep inner resolve and with the help of my agent, Dominick Abel, I found a publisher at last.

Twenty years have passed since *Feel the Fear and Do It Anyway* was first published. It is now available in over 100 countries and has been translated into over 30 languages. And that number continues to grow. From this continuous growth, one can conclude that the words I wrote so long ago are as relevant today as they were then . . . if not more so!

Fear will always be a part of all of our lives in one form or another. And this applies to people everywhere. From the letters of thanks I receive from all over the world, it is clear that no matter who we are . . . no matter where we live . . . no matter what we are experiencing in life, we all feel fear, but fear doesn't need to hold us back from living a rich and beautiful life. We can overcome our fears by regularly using the powerful tools that lie within these pages.

I thank all of you who have let me know in one form or another that *Feel the Fear and Do It Anyway* has made a huge difference in the quality of your lives. It brings me a special feeling of joy and humility to know that I have touched the lives of so many people. It made me realize that trusting my gut and not giving up was a very good thing!

And for you "beginners" who are opening this book for the first time, trust me when I tell you that fear doesn't have to hold you back. You, too, can learn how to push through your fears . . . ALL of your fears . . . with a sense of power, excitement, and love. And that's what this book is all about.

As you will discover, the concepts and tools you are about to learn are meant to be used for a lifetime. Learn them well. And every time a new challenge comes into your life, you need only reach into your "toolbox" and move yourself from the weakest to the strongest part of who you are. As you do, you will be absolutely amazed at the incredible amount of power you hold inside . . . power to love, power to succeed, power to help the world in your own special way. The journey to the best of who you are is exciting and rewarding . . . and I am so happy to be walking right along with you as you take those first important steps.

From my heart to yours,

Susan Jeffers

Introduction
Opening the Door

What is it for you?

Fear of . . .
public speaking
asserting yourself
making decisions
intimacy
changing jobs
being alone
aging
driving
losing a loved one
ending a relationship?

Is it some of the above? All of the above? Perhaps you could add a few more to the list. Never mind . . . join the crowd! Fear seems to be epidemic in our society. We fear beginnings; we fear endings. We fear changing; we fear "staying stuck." We fear success; we fear failure. We fear living; we fear dying.

Whatever the fear, this book will give you the insight and tools to vastly improve your ability to handle any given situation. You will move from a place of pain, paralysis and depression (feelings that often accompany fear) to one of power, energy and excitement.

You may be surprised and encouraged to learn that while inability to deal with fear may look and feel like a psychological problem, in most cases it isn't. I believe it is primarily an educational problem, and that by re-educating the mind, you can accept fear as simply a fact of life rather than a barrier to success. (This should be a relief to all of you out there who have been wondering "What's wrong with me?")

My conviction that fear can be dealt with through re-education came about through my own experiences. When I was younger, I was always run by fear, so it wasn't surprising that for years I hung on to many things in my life that clearly were not working for me.

Part of my problem was the nonstop little voice inside my head that kept telling me, "YOU'D BETTER NOT CHANGE YOUR SITUATION. THERE'S NOTHING ELSE OUT THERE FOR YOU. YOU'LL NEVER MAKE IT ON YOUR OWN." You know the voice I'm talking about – the one that keeps reminding you, "DON'T TAKE A CHANCE YOU MIGHT MAKE A MISTAKE. BOY, WILL YOU BE SORRY!"

My fear never seemed to abate, and I didn't have a moment's peace. Even my doctorate in psychology didn't seem to do me much good. Then one day, as I was dressing for work, I reached the turning point. I happened to glance in the mirror, and I saw an all-too-familiar sight – eyes red and puffy from tears of self-pity. Suddenly rage welled up inside me, and I began shouting at my reflection, "ENOUGH . . . ENOUGH . . . ENOUGH!" I shouted until I had no more energy (or voice) left.

When I stopped, I felt a strange and wonderful sense of relief and calm I had never felt before. Without realizing it at the time, I had gotten in touch with a very powerful part of myself that before that moment I hadn't even known existed. I took another long look in the mirror and smiled as I nodded my head YES. The old familiar voice of doom and gloom was drowned out, at least temporarily, and a new voice had come to the fore – one that spoke of strength and love and joy and all good things. At that moment I knew I was not going to let fear get the best of me. I would find a way to rid myself of the negativism that prevailed in my life. Thus, my odyssey began.

An ancient sage once said, "When the student is ready, the teacher will appear." The student was ready, and teachers appeared from all over the place. I began to read, attend workshops and talk to as many people as would listen. Diligently following every suggestion and lead, I *unlearned* the thinking that had been keeping me a prisoner of my own insecurities. I began to see the world as a less threatening and more joyous place; I started to see myself as someone who had purpose; and I experienced the meaning of love for the first time in my life.

At this point I began to notice many other people struggling with the same barriers I had finally learned to push through – the main barrier being fear. How could I help them? Realizing that the processes that had transformed my life were educational in nature, I was convinced that the same techniques I had used could be taught to anyone, regardless of age, sex or background. I was able to test my theory in the real world by teaching a course at The New School for Social Research, in New York City. Called "Feel the Fear . . . and Do It Anyway," the course was described as follows:

Whenever we take a chance and enter unfamiliar territory or put ourselves into the world in a new way, we experience fear. Very often this fear keeps us from moving ahead with our lives. The trick is to FEEL THE FEAR AND DO IT ANYWAY. Together we will explore the barriers that keep us from experiencing life the way we want to live it. So many of us short-circuit our living by choosing the path that is the most comfortable. Through readings, class discussions and interesting exercises we will learn to identify our excuses for "staying stuck" and develop the techniques for taking control of our own lives.

My experiment with taking the concept of fear out of the realm of therapy and placing it in the area of education was extremely successful. My students were amazed at how shifting their thinking magically reshaped their lives. The concepts worked for them as they had worked for me. And, not surprisingly, my students also became my teachers. They reaffirmed and added to my fund of knowledge as I listened carefully to their wisdom.

Those of you who are reading this book have acknowledged that wherever you are in life at this moment is not exactly the place you want to be. Something needs changing, and until now you haven't been able to take the steps to change it. Whatever your circumstances, you are ready to start taking charge of your life.

I'm not promising that change is easy. It takes courage to mold your life the way you want it to be. There are all sorts of real and imagined obstacles that get in the way. They need not deter you. In your journey through this book you will become familiar with many concepts, exercises and other devices to help you unravel the complexities of fear . . . and thus help you deal with it.
You will learn:

> how it can be impossible to make a mistake or a wrong
>   decision
> how to let go of negative programming
> how it is impossible to be conned
> how to say "yes" to all circumstances in your life

how to raise your level of self-esteem
how to become more assertive
how to connect with the powerhouse within
how to create more love, trust and satisfaction
how to deal with resistance from significant others as you
    take more control of your life
how to experience more enjoyment
how to make your dreams become a reality
how to see yourself as having purpose and meaning

As you read, underline those sections of the book that "speak" to you, so that later you can easily find critical passages to help you face new situations in life. It takes a lot of reinforcement to incorporate new concepts into your behavior, so commit yourself to doing the exercises. The amount of improvement you experience will depend on how much you are willing to participate actively. Also, the more you get involved, the more fun you will have. You will be surprised and pleased at the amount of satisfaction that comes as you take each little step forward.

No matter what degree of insecurity you are feeling, a part of you knows there is a lot of wonderful "stuff" within you just waiting to be let out and NOW is the perfect time for opening the door to the power and love within.

1

What Are You Afraid of . . .
and Why?

I am about to teach another fear class. The classroom is empty. I am waiting for my new group of students to appear. My nervousness about teaching these classes disappeared a long time ago. Not only have I taught it many times, but also I know my students before I meet them. They are like the rest of us: all trying to do the best they can and all uncertain about whether they're good enough. It never varies.

As the students enter the room, I can feel the tension. They sit as far apart from one another as possible, until the seats between must be filled because of lack of space. They don't talk to one another, but sit nervously, expectantly. I love them for their courage to admit that their lives are not working the way they want them to work. And their presence in the class signifies they are ready to do something about it.

I begin by going around the room asking each student to tell the rest of us what he or she is having difficulty confronting in life. Their stories unfold:

Don wants to change his career of fourteen years and follow his dreams of becoming an artist.

Mary Alice is an actress who wants to discover why she finds all kinds of excuses for not attending auditions.

Sarah wants to leave a marriage of fifteen years.

Teddy wants to get over his fear of aging. He is all of thirty-two.

Jean is a senior citizen who wants to confront her doctor; he treats her like a child and never gives her any straight answers.

Patti wants to expand her business, but can't make the required leap into the next step.

Rebecca wants to confront her husband with things that have been bothering her.

Kevin wants to get over a fear of rejection that makes it very difficult to ask a woman for a date.

Laurie wants to know why she is unhappy when she has everything one could possibly want in life.

Richard is retired and feels useless. He fears his life is over.

And so it goes until everyone's story is heard.

I'm fascinated with what happens during the go-around. As each person shares from the heart, the entire atmosphere begins to change. The tension quickly fades and relief is expressed on everyone's face.

First, my students begin to realize they are not the only ones in the world feeling afraid. Second, they begin to see how attractive people become as they open up and share their feelings. Long before the last person has spoken, a feeling of warmth and camaraderie pervades the room. They are strangers no more.

Although the backgrounds and situations of the class members vary greatly, it does not take long for the surface layers of their particular stories to disappear, opening the way for everyone to touch on a very human level. The common denominator is the fact that fear is keeping all of them from experiencing life the way they want to experience it.

The scenario above repeats itself in each fear class I teach. At this point you might be wondering how one course can accommodate all the diverse fears reported by the class members – their needs seem to be so varied. It's true. They do seem varied until we dig a little deeper and look at the underlying cause of all their fears – and everyone else's.

Fear can be broken down into three levels. The first level is the surface story, such as the ones described above. This level of fear can be divided into two types: those that "happen" and those that require action. Here is a partial list of Level 1 fears divided into these types:

Level 1 Fears

Those That "Happen"	*Those Requiring Action*
Aging	Going back to school
Becoming disabled	Making decisions
Retirement	Changing a career
Being alone	Making friends
Children leaving home	Ending or beginning a
Natural disasters	relationship
Loss of financial security	Having a child
Change	Asserting oneself
Dying	Losing weight
War	Being interviewed
Illness	Driving
Losing a loved one	Public speaking
Accidents	Making a mistake
Rape	Intimacy

You might have a few you can add to the list. As I hinted earlier, you wouldn't be alone if you said to yourself, "Some of the above" or even "All of the above." There is a reason for this. One of the insidious qualities of fear is that it tends to permeate many areas of our lives. For example, if you fear making new friends, it then stands to reason you also may fear going to parties, having intimate relationships, applying for jobs, and so on.

This is made clearer by a look at the second layer of fear, which has a very different feel from that of Level 1. Level 2 fears are not situation-oriented; they involve the ego.

Level 2 Fears

Rejection	Being conned
Success	Helplessness
Failure	Disapproval
Being vulnerable	Loss of image

Level 2 fears have to do with *inner states of mind* rather than exterior situations. They reflect your sense of self and your ability to handle this world. This explains why generalized fear takes place. If you are afraid of being rejected, this fear will affect almost every area of your life – friends, intimate relationships, job interviews, and so on. Rejection is rejection – wherever it is found. So you begin to protect yourself, and, as a result, greatly limit yourself. You begin to shut down and close out the world around you. Look over the Level 2 list once again, and you will see how any one of these fears can greatly impact many areas of your life.

Level 3 gets down to the nitty-gritty of the issue: the biggest fear of all – the one that really keeps you stuck. Are you ready?

Level 3 Fears

I CAN'T HANDLE IT!

"That's it? That's the big deal?" you may ask. I know you're disappointed and wanted something much more dramatic than that. But the truth is this:

AT THE BOTTOM OF EVERY ONE OF YOUR FEARS IS SIMPLY THE FEAR THAT YOU CAN'T HANDLE WHATEVER LIFE MAY BRING YOU.

Let's test this. The Level 1 fears translate to:

I can't handle illness.
I can't handle making a mistake.
I can't handle losing my job.
I can't handle getting old.
I can't handle being alone.
I can't handle making a fool out of myself.
I can't handle not getting the job.
I can't handle losing him/her.
I can't handle losing my money . . . etc.

The Level 2 fears translate to:

I can't handle the responsibilities of success.
I can't handle failure.
I can't handle being rejected . . . etc.

Thus Level 3 – simply, "I can't handle it!"

The truth is:

IF YOU KNEW YOU COULD HANDLE ANYTHING THAT CAME YOUR WAY, WHAT WOULD YOU POSSIBLY HAVE TO FEAR?

The answer is: **NOTHING!**

I know you probably are not jumping up and down for joy just yet, but believe me when I tell you I have just given you a great piece of news. What I have just told you means you can handle all your fears without having to control anything in the outside world. This should be a tremendous relief.

You no longer have to control what your mate does, what your friends do, what your children do, or what your boss does. You don't have to control what happens at an interview, what happens at your job, what happens in your new career, what happens to your money, or what happens in the stock market.

ALL YOU HAVE TO DO TO DIMINISH YOUR FEAR IS TO DEVELOP MORE TRUST IN YOUR ABILITY TO HANDLE WHATEVER COMES YOUR WAY!

I am belaboring the point because it is so critical. From this moment on, every time you feel afraid, remind yourself that it is simply because you are not feeling good enough about yourself. Then proceed to use one or more of the tools in this book to help build yourself up. You have your task clearly mapped out for you. There is no reason for confusion.

I've often been asked to explain why we have so little trust in ourselves. I don't really know the answer to that. I know that some fear is instinctual and healthy and keeps us alert to trouble. The rest – the part that holds us back from personal growth – is inappropriate and destructive, and perhaps can be blamed on our conditioning.

In all my life I have never heard a mother call out to her child as he or she goes off to school, "Take a lot of risks today, darling." She is more likely to convey to her child, "Be careful, darling." This "Be careful" carries with it a double message: "The world is really dangerous out there" . . . *and* . . . "you won't be able to handle it." What Mom is really saying, of course, is, "If something happens to you, *I* won't be able to handle it." You see, she is only passing on her lack of trust in *her* ability to handle what comes her way.

I can remember wanting desperately to have a two-wheel bicycle and my mother's refusal to buy me one. Her answer to my pleas was always the same: "I love you too much. I don't want anything to happen to you." I translated this to mean: "You are not competent enough to handle a two-wheel bike." Having become older and wiser, I realize now that she was really saying: "If anything happens to you, I will fall apart."

This overprotective mother of mine was once in intensive care after serious surgery, with tubes down her nose and her throat. When I was told it was time for me to leave, I whispered in her ear – not knowing if she could hear me – that I loved her and would be back later. As I was walking toward the door, I heard a small, weak voice behind me saying – you guessed it – "Be careful." Even in her anesthetic stupor, she was sending me admonitions of doom and gloom. And I know she typifies the great percentage of mothers out there. Considering how many "be careful"s our parents bombarded us with, it is amazing we even manage to walk out the front door!

Apart from such seemingly obvious connections, the cause of our fear quite possibly lies elsewhere. But does it really matter where our self-doubts come from? I believe not. It is not my approach to analyze the whys and wherefores of troublesome areas of the mind. It is often impossible to figure out what the actual causes of negative patterns are, and even if we did know, the knowing doesn't necessarily change them. I believe that if something is troubling you, simply start from where you are and take the action necessary to change it.

In this case, you know that you don't like the fact that lack of trust in yourself is stopping you from getting what you want out of life. Knowing this creates a very clear, even laserlike, focus on what needs to be changed. You don't have to scatter your energy wondering why. It doesn't matter. What matters is that you begin now to develop your trust in yourself, until you reach the point where you will be able to say:

WHATEVER HAPPENS TO ME, GIVEN ANY SITUATION, I CAN HANDLE IT!

I can hear the doubting Thomases out there saying, "Oh, come on now, how do you handle paralysis, or the death of a child, or cancer?" I understand your skepticism. Remember that I was once a doubting Thomas myself. Just read on and let the book unfold. Give yourself a winning chance by using the tools provided throughout this book. As you do, you will find yourself coming closer and closer to such a high level of self-confidence that you will ultimately begin to realize that you can handle *anything* that comes your way. Never let these three little words out of your mind – possibly the most important three little words you'll ever hear:

I'LL HANDLE IT!

2

Can't You Make It Go Away?

Janet's still waiting for the fear to go away. She had always planned to return to college once her children were in school, but she now notices it's been four years since her youngest child entered first grade. New excuses have popped up since that time: "I want to be here when the children come home from school"; "We really don't have the money"; "My husband will feel neglected."

Although it is true that certain logistics would have to be worked out, that is not the reason for her hesitation. In fact, her husband is willing to help her in any way he can. He is concerned about her restlessness, and often encourages her to fulfill her lifelong dream of becoming a fashion designer.

Each time Janet thinks about calling the local college to set up an interview, something stops her. "When I'm not so frightened, then I'll make the call"; "When I feel a little better about myself, then I'll make the call." Most likely Janet is going to wait a very long time.

The problem is that her thinking is all mixed up. The logic she uses automatically programs her for failure. She will never break the fear barrier until she is made aware of her faulty thinking; she simply does not "see" what is obvious to those who are out there doing it.

Nor did I until I was forced to. Before my divorce from my first husband, I was rather like a child, allowing him to take over the practicalities of my life. After my divorce, I had no choice but to start doing things on my own. Small things, such as fixing the vacuum cleaner all by myself, brought me enormous satisfaction. The first night I invited people to my home for dinner as a single person was a monumental leap. The day I booked tickets for my first trip without a man was a day for celebration.

As I began to *do* things on my own, I began to taste the deliciousness of an emerging self-confidence. It wasn't all comfortable – in fact, a lot of it was extremely uncomfortable. I felt like a child learning to walk and falling frequently. But with each step I felt a little surer of my ability to handle my life.

As my confidence grew, I kept waiting for the fear to go away. Yet each time I ventured out into a new territory, I felt frightened and unsure of myself. "Well," I told myself "just keep putting yourself out there. *Eventually* the fear will go away." It never did! One day a light bulb went on in my head as I suddenly realized the following "truth":

TRUTH 1
THE FEAR WILL NEVER GO AWAY
AS LONG AS I CONTINUE TO GROW.

As long as I continued to push out into the world, as long as I continued to stretch my capabilities, as long as I continued to take new risks in making my dreams come true, I was going to experience fear. What a revelation! Like Janet, and so many of you reading this book, I had grown up waiting for the fear to go away before I took any chances. "When I am no longer afraid . . . then!" For most of my life, I had played the WHEN/THEN game. And it never worked.

Once again you are probably not jumping up and down with joy. I am aware that this revelation is not exactly one you wanted to hear. If you are like my students, you were hoping that my words of wisdom would miraculously make your fears go away. I'm sorry to say it doesn't work that way. On the other hand, rather than think of it as a disappointment, consider it a relief that you no longer have to work so hard on getting rid of the fear. It isn't going to go away! Not to worry. As you build your confidence in yourself with the exercises suggested herein, your relationship with fear will dramatically alter.

Not long after discovering Truth 1, I made another important discovery that contributed enormously to my growth:

TRUTH 2
THE ONLY WAY TO GET RID OF THE FEAR OF DOING SOMETHING IS TO GO OUT AND DO IT.

This sounds contradictory to Truth 1, yet it isn't. Fear of *particular* situations dissolved when I finally confronted them. The "doing it" comes *before* the fear goes away.

I can illustrate this by recounting my first teaching experience when I was studying for my doctorate. I was not much older than my students and I was teaching a subject in which I had dubious expertise – the psychology of aging. I anticipated the first class period with a tremendous sense of dread. During the three days prior to the class, my stomach felt like it was on a roller coaster. I had prepared eight hours of work for a one-hour class. I had handwritten enough material for three lectures. None of this took away my fear. When the first day of class finally arrived, I felt like I was being sent to the guillotine. As I stood in front of my students, I could feel my heart pounding and my knees shaking. Somehow I got through that class period – not ecstatically looking forward to the second one the following week.

Thankfully, things were easier the next time. (If not, I

might have left teaching permanently!) I started to become familiar with the faces in the classroom and connected some of the names to the faces. The third class was better than the second, as I started to relax and go with the flow of the students. By our sixth session I was actually looking forward to standing in front of my class. The interaction with my students was stimulating and challenging. One day, as I was approaching that once dreaded classroom, I realized I was no longer afraid. My fear had turned into sweet anticipation.

I had to teach a number of different courses before I was comfortable walking into class without voluminous notes. But there did come a day when all I had in my hand was a one-page outline of what I intended to cover that period. I realized how far I had come. I had felt the fear . . . and done it anyway. As a result, I got rid of my fear of teaching. Yet, when I took my teaching into the television arena, once again I experienced fear, until my "doing it" often enough eliminated my fear of appearing on television. So it goes.

Another part of the WHEN/THEN game I used to play had to do with self-esteem. "When I feel better about myself . . . then I'll do it." This is another mix-up in the order of reality. I kept thinking that if I could improve my self-image, then the fear would go away and I could start accomplishing things. I didn't know exactly *how* my self-image was going to improve. Perhaps by my growing older and wiser, or through feedback from other people, or a miracle would make me feel wonderful about myself. I actually bought myself a belt buckle that read I'M TERRIFIC, thinking that through osmosis I'd get the message.

Maybe all those things did help a little. What really made the difference, however, was the sense of accomplishment I felt in pushing through fear and doing things on my own. Finally, this became clear:

TRUTH 3
THE ONLY WAY TO FEEL BETTER ABOUT MYSELF IS TO GO OUT . . . AND DO IT.

The "doing it" comes *before* the feeling better about yourself. When you make something happen, not only does the fear of the situation go away, but also you get a big bonus: you do a lot toward building your self-confidence. It's fairly predictable, however, that when you've finally mastered something and gotten rid of the fear, it will feel so good you will decide there is something else out there you want to accomplish, and – guess what! The fear begins again as you prepare to meet a new challenge.

Through all the workshops and seminars I attended in my early stages of dealing with fear, I was relieved to learn something else that made me feel infinitely better about myself:

TRUTH 4
NOT ONLY AM I GOING TO EXPERIENCE FEAR WHENEVER I'M ON UNFAMILIAR TERRITORY, BUT SO IS EVERYONE ELSE.

I said to myself: *"You mean all those people out there that I've been envying because they're not afraid to move ahead with their lives have really been afraid? Why didn't somebody tell me!?"* I guess I never asked. I was sure I was the only person out there feeling so inadequate. It was such a relief to realize I was not alone in this. I had the rest of the world to keep me company.

I remember a newspaper article I read years ago about Ed Koch, the seemingly fearless mayor of New York City. The article told of how he had to learn a tap-dance routine with the cast of a Broadway show for a publicity event. His teacher reported that the mayor was scared to death. This was hard to believe! A man who had often faced crowds of angry people, who had made many difficult decisions affecting millions of lives, who had put himself before the public in his race to be mayor . . . and he was afraid to learn a simple tap dance!

If one is aware of the Fear Truths, the mayor's fear will not come as a surprise. Tap dancing was an activity that tested him in a new way, and of course he would be frightened. Once he practiced and mastered the routine, the fear would go away, and his confidence in himself would be heightened – he could put another feather in his cap, so to speak. That's simply the way it works – *for all of us.* By virtue of our all being human, we share the same feelings. Fear is no exception.

Many stories similar to Mayor Koch's appear in newspapers, magazines, books and on television. Until you are in touch with the Fear Truths, you will hear about and read and see these stories and not notice the underlying principles operating. You may never relate the experiences of others, especially those of celebrities, to your life. You may think they are lucky because they aren't afraid to put themselves out there. *Not so!* They had to push through a tremendous amount of fear to get where they are today . . . and they are still pushing.

Those who have successfully dealt with fear all their lives seem to have known, consciously or unconsciously, the message in this book: You must feel the fear . . . and do it anyway. A very successful friend of mine, a self-made man who allowed nothing to stop him along the way, pondered the title of my course one day, nodded, and said, "Yes, I guess that is the way I've always lived my life, without consciously realizing that's what I've been doing. I can't remember not being afraid, but it never occurred to me that fear would prevent me from taking the risks necessary to get what I wanted. I just went ahead and did what I had to do to make my ideas work – despite the fear."

If you have not been successful in dealing with fear, you probably never learned the Fear Truths, and interpreted fear as a signal to retreat rather than as a green light to move ahead. You have tended to play those WHEN/THEN games I mentioned earlier. All you have to do to find a way out of your self-imposed prison is to retrain your thinking.

A first step in retraining your thinking is to say the Fear Truths at least ten times a day for the next month. As you will shortly discover, retraining faulty thinking takes constant repetition. *Knowing* the Fear Truths is not enough. You have to keep feeding them to yourself until they become a part of your being – until you start to reverse your behavior and move *toward* your desired goals, rather than retreat. There will be more later about why repetition is important. For now, just trust me and repeat the Fear Truths over and over again.

Before you begin, however, I'd like to add one very important Fear Truth to the list. You might already have been asking yourself, "Why should I put myself through all the discomfort that comes with taking risks? Why don't I just go on living my life the way I've been living it?" You might find my answer to that question surprising. It is:

TRUTH 5
PUSHING THROUGH FEAR IS LESS FRIGHTENING THAN LIVING WITH THE UNDERLYING FEAR THAT COMES FROM A FEELING OF HELPLESSNESS.

Read it again. I know it's hard to take in at first. It says that no matter how "secure" any of us feel in the little cocoon we have built for ourselves, we live, consciously or unconsciously, with the fear that the day of reckoning will eventually come.

The more helpless we feel, the more severe is the undercurrent of dread that comes with knowing there are situations in life over which we have no control – such as the death of a spouse or the loss of a job. We find ourselves becoming obsessive about possible catastrophes. "What if . . . ?" Fear permeates our lives. That is the irony of Fear Truth 5: people who refuse to take risks live with a feeling of dread that is far more severe than what they would feel if they took the risks necessary to make them less helpless – only they don't know it!

I can illustrate with the case of Janice, a middle-aged housewife, who "planned" her life in such a way as to avoid risk-taking as much as possible. She married a successful businessman who handled both their lives. Janice allowed this situation because it was more comfortable for her never to put herself on the line. But, as the saying goes, "Life is what happens when we've made other plans!" At the age of fifty-three, her husband, Dick, had a stroke, which left him partially disabled. One day she was totally *taken* care of and the next she was totally *taking* care of.

The transition wasn't easy. After fighting the rage of "Why did this happen to me?" she started to accept the fact that she was now in charge of both her own and her husband's survival. Numbed, she went through the motions of learning his business, handling decisions regarding his health, and waking up every morning with the understanding that it was now up to her. After a while, the numbness left, the fog cleared, and she discovered a profound sense of peace she had never experienced before. She started to realize the heavy price she had paid to be taken care of.

Prior to her husband's stroke, Janice's thinking had been permeated with the phrase "what if." She always worried about the future, never enjoying her todays. She had lived with the underlying dread "My God, what if something happened to him?" She had often remarked to her friends, "I hope I die before he does. I couldn't live without him." And she thought she couldn't – which is a less than satisfactory way to go through life. This all changed as she found strength she never thought she had. She now knows the answer to her question "what if." The answer is: "I'll handle it!"

Janice had never realized she was living with terror all her life until that terror disappeared. The new fears were nothing compared to her old fears about survival. Her husband has now recovered enough for them to live a satisfying life together. He, too, has faced one of his biggest fears – that of becoming disabled. He got the answer to his question "what if," which was also "I'll handle it." They both handled it beautifully. In fact, through this experience they learned the real meaning of love.

By now you've gotten the picture. We can't escape fear. We can only transform it into a companion that accompanies us in all our exciting adventures; it is not an anchor holding us transfixed in one spot. Some people have told me they are never afraid, but when I question them, they reveal that we are just differing on semantics. Yes, they feel nervous or anxious sometimes – they simply never labeled it fear.

As far as I know, everyone feels fear as he or she moves forward through life. It is absolutely possible that there are some evolved souls in this world who never experience fear and I have not met them. If I do, I promise I will become their avid student and report back to you with their secrets. You see, I "know" on some deep level there is nothing to fear. It's the surface level that needs convincing. In the meantime I've learned to "feel the fear . . . and do it anyway!" As I do, whether I feel the fear or not becomes irrelevant. My life will work in either case . . . as will yours.

Five Truths about Fear

1. The fear will never go away as long as I continue to grow.
2. The only way to get rid of the fear of doing something is to go out . . . and do it.
3. The only way to feel better about myself is to go out . . . and do it.
4. Not only am I going to experience fear whenever I'm on unfamiliar territory, but so is everyone else.
5. Pushing through fear is less frightening than living with the underlying fear that comes from a feeling of helplessness.

3

From Pain to Power

The last chapter revealed a critical insight indeed, and that is:

IF EVERYBODY FEELS FEAR WHEN
APPROACHING
SOMETHING TOTALLY NEW IN LIFE,
YET SO MANY ARE OUT THERE "DOING IT"
DESPITE THE FEAR,
THEN WE MUST CONCLUDE THAT
FEAR IS NOT THE PROBLEM.

Obviously, the real issue has nothing to do with the fear itself, but, rather, how we *hold* the fear. For some, the fear is totally irrelevant. For others, it creates a state of paralysis. The former hold their fear from a position of power (choice, energy and action), and the latter hold it from a position of pain (helplessness, depression and paralysis).

The chart on the next page illustrates this concept.

From this it can be seen that the secret in handling fear is to move yourself from a position of pain to a position of power. The fact that you have the fear then becomes irrelevant.

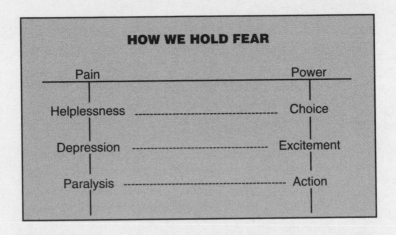

Let's talk about the word "power." Some people say that they do not like the concept of power and want no part of it. It is true that in our world the word "power" has some negative overtones. It often implies control over others, and, unfortunately, is often misused.

The kind of power I am talking about is entirely different. In fact, it makes you *less* manipulative of those around you, and certainly more loving. I am talking about *power within the self.* This means power over your perceptions of the world, power over how you react to situations in your life, power to do what is necessary for your own self-growth, power to create joy and satisfaction in your life, power to act and power to love.

This kind of power has nothing to do with anyone else. It is not egomania, but a healthy self-love. In fact, egomaniacs have absolutely no feeling of power – thus their compelling need to control those around them. Their lack of power leaves them perpetually in a state of fear, since their survival depends on the outside world. No one is more unloving than a person who can't own his or her own power. Such people spend their lives trying to pull it out of everyone else. Their need creates all sorts of manipulative behavior.

The kind of power I'm talking about leaves you free, since you don't expect the rest of the world to fill you up. It's not the ability to get someone else to do what you want them to do. It's the ability to get yourself to do what you want to do. If you do not own this kind of power, you lose your sense of peace. You are in a very vulnerable place.

I have found that women are more put off than men are by the concept of power, for obvious reasons. Men have been conditioned to believe that to be powerful is good. Women have been conditioned to believe that to be powerful is un-feminine and unattractive. It is my experience that nothing could be farther from the truth.

A self-assured woman who is in control of her life draws like a magnet. She is so filled with positive energy that people want to be around her. Yet it is only when she has become powerful within herself that she can become authentic and loving to those around her. *The truth is that love and power go together.* With power, one can really begin to open up the heart. With no power, love is distorted.

For the women reading this book, a good antidote to any inner conflict between power and femininity is to repeat to yourself at least twenty-five times each morning, noon and night:

I AM POWERFUL AND I AM LOVED.

And:

I AM POWERFUL AND I AM LOVING.

An energizing variation is:

I AM POWERFUL AND I LOVE IT!

Say these three statements aloud right now. Feel the energy the words convey. Their constant repetition will help make the concepts of power and love more compatible and certainly more comfortable.

Now that I've explained the kind of power I'm talking

about, let's explore how to use the Pain-to-Power concept in daily life.

The first step is to create a Pain-to-Power Chart, as follows:

PAIN-TO-POWER CHART

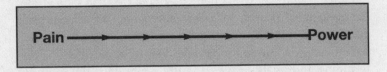

As we look at the Pain-to-Power continuum, most of us can place ourselves somewhere in the middle of the chart. We're not totally incapacitated by our fears, but we're not exactly feeling a great sense of power and excitement, nor are we quickly sprinting to our goals. We seem to be taking the arduous route over the mountain carrying two suitcases and a watermelon rather than flying on the wings of eagles. As an ancient sage once said, "The pathway is smooth. Why do you throw rocks before you?"

Using the Pain-to-Power Chart as a frame of reference, you can begin to clear the rocks in front of you. The following steps will help in the clearing process:

1. Draw an enlargement of the Pain-to-Power Chart and place it on your wall. Just the simple act of making the enlargement will make you feel a little more powerful. You are already taking action! Remember that much of the trick of moving from pain to power is taking action, ACTION IS VERY POWERFUL! Once the chart is on your wall it will serve as a constant reminder of where you want to go in life – from pain to power. *Awareness* is half the battle. Having the chart physically present will also help you motivate yourself to keep moving in the right direction.

2. Just to keep you from taking yourself too seriously, you might want to write somewhere on your chart "Angels fly because they take themselves lightly." I heard this quote by Gilbert K. Chesterton a long time ago, and it still makes me smile. It constantly reminds me that you can drop an awful lot of excess baggage if you learn to play with life instead of fight it.

3. Put a pin at the place on the chart where you see yourself situated at this moment in your life. Are you in the middle, where you sometimes feel depressed and paralyzed and at other times feel more in control? Or do you definitely find yourself on the far left side, where there is little you are able to do to pull yourself out of the rut? Or perhaps you are already on the right side, where most of the time you feel you are really moving ahead with your life, with only a few areas that need to be worked on. I doubt that anyone reading this book has reached their goal of attaining absolute power over the self. Even the Buddhas have their days! There are always new experiences that challenge a sense of personal power.

4. Each day look at the chart and ask yourself, "Do I see myself at the same place, or have I moved?" Move the pin accordingly.

5. If you keep in mind the direction you want to go, it will help you make decisions about what you are doing in your life. Before you take any action in life, ask yourself: "Is this action moving me to a more powerful place?" If it isn't, you will think twice about doing it. *A word of caution:* If you go ahead anyway, knowing the action will keep you in a position of pain, don't get angry with yourself about it. Just notice where you are not taking responsibility. The next time, you can make a different decision. Use your "mistakes" as learning experiences. Remember that each time you get angry at yourself for an action you have taken, you keep yourself on the side of pain.

6. Make your use of the chart fun. Having it as a game keeps you light about the situation. If you have children, they can create their own charts, and you can make a family game out of the experience of growing.

7. You might want to make different charts for different areas of your life. To be really powerful, you need to be in charge of all aspects of your life – your work, relationships, environment, body, and so on. Often people are very powerful in some parts of their lives and pathetic in others. For example, I am very powerful in terms of my career, but need to work on the area of exercise.

Note that your movement on the chart is determined only by your own intuitive sense of how far you are progressing in gaining more power in your life. No one else can judge that, though they may try. Although your life may look exactly the same to the outside world, it is your own sense of internal peace and growth that determines where you are on the chart. It is, totally, a feeling within.

You may wonder if you really need to go to such lengths to get yourself moving. Trust me – you do! In the beginning, you need all the gimmicks you can get to remind you of where you want to go. You don't become powerful without concentrating on power. As you must have figured out by now, simply knowing what to do does not mean that you do it, or, for that matter, even remember it.

To help you on your Pain-to-Power path, it's important that you begin to develop a Pain-to-Power Vocabulary. The way you use words has a tremendous impact on the quality of your life. Certain words are destructive; others are empowering. Choose to move to a Pain-to-Power Vocabulary as follows:

PAIN-TO-POWER VOCABULARY

Pain ➤ ➤ ➤ ➤ Power	
I can't	I won't
I should	I could
It's not my fault	I'm totally responsible
It's a problem	It's an opportunity
I'm never satisfied	I want to learn and grow
Life's a struggle	Life's an adventure
I hope	I know
If only	Next time
What will I do?	I know I can handle it
It's terrible	It's a learning experience

"I can't" implies you have no control over your life, whereas "*I won't*" puts a situation in the realm of choice. From this moment on, strike "I can't" from your vocabulary. When you give your subconscious the message "I can't," your subconscious really believes you and registers on its computer: WEAK . . . WEAK . . . WEAK. Your subconscious believes only what it hears, not what is true. You might be saying "I can't" simply to get out of a dinner invitation – such as, "I can't come to dinner tonight. I have to prepare for tomorrow's meeting," but your subconscious is registering, "He's weak!" In fact, "I can't come to dinner" is an untruth. The truth is "I *can* come to dinner, but I *am choosing* to do something that has a higher priority at the moment." But the subconscious can't discern the difference and is still registering "weak."

Although you may want to be more delicate to your host than to utter the above statement, you can still stay away from the words "I can't." "I'd love to come to dinner, but I have a meeting tomorrow that's important to me. I'll feel better walking in totally prepared. So I'll pass for tonight and hope you'll invite me again." That statement has truth, integrity and power. The subconscious hears you stating your priorities with clarity and choosing the outcome that serves your own growth. Choosing this way doesn't leave you the helpless victim of your meeting.

"I should" is another loser. It, too, implies that you have no choices in life. "*I could*" is more powerful. "I could visit my mother, but I'm choosing to go to the movies today." This puts things in the realm of choice instead of obligation. "I can visit my mother or I can go to the movies. I think I'll choose my mother today." "Shoulds" bring on guilt and upset – totally draining emotions. Your power is taken away every time you utter the words "I should."

"It's not my fault" is another beauty. Once again, you look helpless. It's better to take responsibility for whatever happens to you in life than always to be the victim. "It's not my fault I got sick"; "It's not my fault I lost the job." If you are willing to take responsibility, then you might see what you can change in the future. Relative to illness, say, "*I'm totally responsible* for my illness. Let's see what I can do to prevent it from happening again. I can change my diet. I can reduce stress. I can stop smoking. I can get enough sleep." And so on. Watch how powerful you become! The same occurs with the lost job. If you are responsible, you can be better prepared the next time; you can find out what made the difference. You are in control. Each time you find yourself in better control of your life you are moving to a position of power, which will ultimately reduce your fear level.

"It's a problem" is another deadening phrase. It's heavy and negative. "*It's an opportunity*" opens the door to growth. Each time you can see the gift in life's obstacles, you can handle difficult situations in a rewarding way. Each time you have the opportunity to stretch your capacity to handle the world, the more powerful you become.

"I hope" is another victim's phrase. *"I know"* has far more power.

> I hope I will get a job.
> I know I will get a job.

What a difference! The first sets you up for worry and sleepless nights. The second has peace and calm about it.

"If only" is boring. You can hear the whine behind it. *"Next time"* implies that you have learned from the situation and will put the learning to use another time. For example, "If only I hadn't said that to Tom" can be restated, "I've learned Tom is sensitive about this issue. Next time, *I'll* be more sensitive."

"What will I do?" Again you can hear the whine and the fear implied in these words. You, like everyone else, have incredible sources of power within that you haven't used before. It would serve you to say to yourself, *"I know I'll handle it.* I have nothing to worry about." Instead of, "I've lost my job! What will I do?" try "I've lost my job. I know I'll handle it."

"It's terrible" is bandied around in the most inappropriate circumstances. For example, "I lost my wallet. Isn't that terrible?" What's so terrible about losing a wallet? It's certainly an inconvenience; it's hardly terrible. "I gained two pounds. Isn't that terrible?" It's hardly terrible to gain two pounds. Yet that's the way we talk about trivia in our lives. And our subconscious is registering, DISASTER . . . DISASTER . . . DISASTER. Replace "it's terrible" with *"It's a learning experience."*

While you might feel more justified in saying "It's terrible" if a loved one has cancer, keep in mind that this attitude takes away your power to deal with the situation. There are many who have learned important things from the experience. I know, because I am one of those people.

My experience of cancer taught me many wonderful things about myself and the people around me. Most important, I learned how much I was loved. I saw a tender side of my fiancé, now my husband, I had never seen before, and our love deepened immeasurably. We stopped taking each other for granted. Also, I have changed my life in many positive ways. I've become a much more aware eater. I've learned how to eliminate the anger, resentment and stress that was very much a part of my daily life prior to my illness. My cancer experience has given my husband and me an opportunity to contribute something to this world. I wrote a very positive article about my mastectomy, which I know has been of value to many men and women. My husband and I have appeared on television together to relate our experience, bringing reassurance to viewers. So you see, cancer *can* be a great learning experience and an opportunity to give.

You get the picture. Begin eliminating the terribles, can'ts, problems, struggles, and so on from your vocabulary. Maybe these semantic differences seem trivial, but I assure you they are not. Not only does your sense of yourself change with a more powerful vocabulary, so also does your presence in the world. People who display an inner strength are treated differently from those who come across as weak. The more powerfully you speak, the more you will be a force in the world around you.

As you begin to monitor your vocabulary, you can also bring more power into your life by *expanding your comfort zone*. What does that mean?

Most of us operate within a zone that feels right, outside of which we are uncomfortable. For example, we might spend $75 dollars for a pair of shoes, but $100 would make us nervous. We might be willing to initiate friendships with people at the office who are at our level in the company, but would be uncomfortable doing so with one of the higher-ups. We might go to the local deli when eating alone, but would feel really uncomfortable in a luxurious restaurant all by ourselves. We might ask for a $5,000 raise, but $7,000 would make us cringe. We may charge $30 an hour for our services, but we don't feel we are worth $35. And so on.

For each one of us that zone of comfort is different, but whether we are aware of it or not, all of us – rich or poor, low or high on the totem pole, male or female – make decisions based on the confines of that comfortable space.

I suggest that each day you do something that widens that space for you. Call someone you are intimidated to call, buy a pair of shoes that costs more than you would ever have paid in the past, ask for something you want that you have been too frightened to ask for before. Take a risk a day – one small or bold stroke that will make you feel great once you've done it. Even if it doesn't work out the way you wanted it to, at least you've tried. You didn't sit back . . . powerless. Watch what starts to happen when you expand your comfort zone:

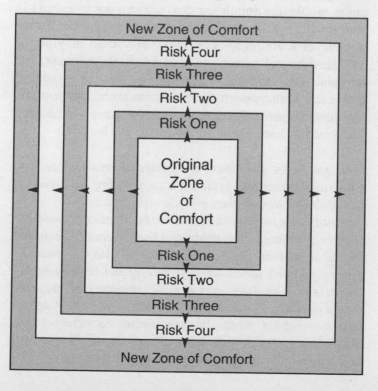

As the drawing shows, with each risk you take, each time you move out of what feels comfortable, you become more powerful. Your whole life expands to take in more of what there is in this world to experience. As your power builds, so does your confidence, so that stretching your comfort zone becomes easier and easier, despite any fear you may be experiencing. The magnitude of the risks you take also expands. In the beginning you may sign up for one evening course after being out of school for fifteen years. Ultimately you may enroll to get your graduate degree. You will be expanding . . . opening up . . . becoming bigger . . . but all at your own pace. As long as you are taking those risks – no matter how small – you are moving yourself to the right on the Pain-to-Power Chart.

Each night before you go to bed, plan the risk you are going to take the following day. Close your eyes, and in your mind's eye, practice doing it. Make your visualization as clear as you possibly can. Also, as you go through the day, be aware of where you find yourself hesitating, and start planning your future risks based on these observations. If you can push through the hesitation at the moment you recognize it, great. Remember that the more you expand your comfort zone, the more powerful you become.

PLEASE NOTE: *The risks I am talking about do not include physically dangerous acts, such as speeding in a car, or taking drugs. Nor do they include risks that infringe on the rights of other people, such as making a pass at someone's mate or, for that matter, robbing a bank. Not only could you end up unpopular, dead or in prison, but also you would be moving yourself far to the left side of the Pain-to-Power Chart. These kinds of acts are not empowering, because they do not have any integrity or love – for one's self or others – behind them. Without these ingredients, it is impossible to build your sense of self-worth. Hence your ability to handle fear would be greatly diminished.*

So take only those risks each day that build your sense of self-worth. These are the risks that enhance your ability to deal with your fears. EXPAND! EXPAND! EXPAND!

Whether it feels like it or not, you already have more power than you could ever have imagined. We all have. When I speak of going from pain to power, I am not talking about pulling the power in from any outside source. Inside of you, just waiting to emerge, is an incredible source of energy, which is more than sufficient for you to create a joyful and satisfying life. It isn't magic. It is only a process of tapping the energy already there, though you are not aware of it.

The exercises contained in this book are designed to lead you to this great source of power. Whether you do them or not is a good clue as to whether you are willing at this time to accept all that is within you. If you are not, don't berate yourself. Just make a commitment to keep working toward it. One way to do this is to read and reread this book and other personal-growth books until you rid yourself of the negative belief systems that are keeping you stuck in your powerlessness. Most of us are filled with old conditioning that is keeping us weak. It takes constant repetition for newer and healthier patterns to take hold.

You are innately designed to use your personal power. When you don't, you experience helplessness, paralysis and depression – which is your clue that something is not working as it could. You, like all of us, deserve everything that is wonderful and exciting in life. And those feelings emerge only when you get in touch with your powerful self.

4

Whether You Want It
or Not . . . It's Yours

Are you a "victim," or are you taking responsibility for your life? So many of us *think* we are taking responsibility for our own lives when we simply are not. The "victim" mentality is very subtle and takes many forms. Once you understand the concepts in this chapter you will better understand the dynamics of handling fear.

The idea of taking responsibility for your own life is probably not totally new to you. For years you have been bombarded with the message: TAKE RESPONSIBILITY FOR YOUR OWN LIFE.

But I am convinced that most of us do not really understand what that means.

To most of us "independent" people, it has meant that we should get a job, earn enough money to support ourselves and not depend on anyone else for our survival. That may or may not be part of it (I know many "dependent" people who understand the secret of taking responsibility for their experience of life), but it certainly doesn't hit the heart of the issue, which is much bigger, yet more invisible, than that. Let's look at a few examples.

Edward is an extremely wealthy, high-powered executive who lives in a constant state of anxiety. When I suggested that he get some professional help, he responded that if the people in his life would change, everything would be fine. If only his wife would be more loving, if only his boss wasn't always leaning on him, and if only his son would stop taking drugs – then he'd be fine. He feels there is no reason for him to get help; it's all *their* fault. Is he taking responsibility for his experience of life? Absolutely not!

Mara is, objectively, sitting on top of the world. She has a great job, lives in a lovely apartment, has many friends and lovers. Her continual complaint is about her ex-husband: he is making her life miserable, he has always been unfair to her, he never pays child support. Also, her son is turning against her and accusing her of being selfish . . . and on . . . and on . . . and on. Is she taking responsibility for her experience of life? Absolutely not!

I know many single or divorced people who are constantly complaining about their ex-husbands or their ex-wives, their bosses, their loneliness, the lousy singles scene, and so on. I know many married people who are constantly lamenting about their children, their lack of money, their lack of communication with their spouses, and so on. Are any of them really taking responsibility for their experience of life? Not at all!

They are all, in some way, playing the role of victim. They have given their power to someone or something else. Keep in mind that when you give away your power, you move farther and farther to the left side of the Pain-to-Power Chart, and as a result you become paralyzed in your attempts to deal with fear.

On a more obvious level, if you're in a job you hate, if you're single and you want to be married, if you're in a lousy relationship and want to get out, if your daughter is making you gray before your time, and if, generally speaking, nothing seems to go the way you want it to go, you are also playing the role of victim. No wonder you feel fearful – victims are powerless!

THE TRUTH IS YOU REALLY ARE IN CONTROL – IN TOTAL CONTROL. For some reason, you are consciously or unconsciously choosing to be in that lousy job, you are choosing to hate the single life, you are choosing to stay in a destructive relationship, you are choosing to let your daughter drive you crazy, you are choosing to sabotage anything good in your life . . . or whatever else it may be for you. I know it is difficult to accept the fact that you are the cause of the feelings that take away your joy in life. It is very upsetting when you begin to see yourself as your own worst enemy. On the other hand, *this realization is your biggest blessing.* If you know you can create your own misery, it stands to reason that you can also create your own joy.

Since taking responsibility for your experience of life is an elusive concept, I will explain the components of a more powerful way of living. Note that I have been careful not to ask you to believe that you are responsible for all your experiences *in* life (although there are some who would argue that you are). Rather, I ask you to believe you are the cause of all your experiences *of* life, meaning that you are the cause of your *reactions* to everything that happens to you. There is a lot more about this in the next chapter and in Chapter 9.

As you read the following seven definitions of taking responsibility, keep remembering that whenever you are not taking responsibility, you put yourself in a position of pain, and hence decrease your ability to handle the fear in your life.

1. *Taking responsibility means never blaming anyone else for anything you are being, doing, having or feeling.* "Never?" you say. "But this time it really is his fault" (or her fault, or the boss's fault, or my son's fault, or the economy's fault, or my mother's fault, or my father's fault, or my friend's fault!). "Really, it is!" If I missed anyone or anything, just add it to the list. Until you fully understand that *you*, and no one else, create what goes on in your head, you will never be in control of your life. Here are a few scenarios I've heard in my classes and the questions these individuals had to ask themselves before they were able to move to a more powerful place.

Madeline
"Well, it certainly was my husband's fault that the last twenty-five years of my life have been so miserable!"

Why did you choose to stay? Why couldn't you take in any of the nice things he did for you instead of only finding fault? Why are you so filled with anger that he finds it impossible to communicate with you?

David
"Well, it certainly was my son's fault that I have gray hair, from worrying about him."

Why didn't you believe that he would find his own way? Why did you always need to rescue him? Why did you make him so much an extension of yourself that you expected too much from him? Why couldn't you just let him be who he is?

Tony
"Well, it certainly is the fault of the job market that I'm stuck in this lousy job."

Why can't you see that others are finding jobs even if the job market is so poor? Why are you not creating more satisfaction in the job you already have? Why aren't you even trying to find a new job? Why are you not asking for what you want in the job you are already in, instead of constantly complaining that nothing is right? Why aren't you committed to doing the best you can do?

Alice

"Well, it certainly is my children's fault that I'm not moving ahead in a career."

Why haven't you noticed that others with children are going ahead with their careers, and their children are doing fine? Why haven't you taken up your husband's offer to help you with the kids if you want to work? Why haven't you made any effort to gain some skills that would really help you get a job you would love?

If you are feeling some pain from identifying with any of the stories above, good. It simply pinpoints an area on which you have to work. The point to remember is that when you blame any outside force for any of your experience of life, you are literally giving away all your power and thus creating pain, paralysis and depression.

2. *Taking responsibility means not blaming yourself.* I know this sounds contradictory, but it is not. *Anything* that takes away your power or your pleasure makes you a victim. Don't make yourself a victim of yourself!

For some, this is more difficult than not blaming others. Once you become aware that you have created so much of your unhappiness, you may have a tendency to punish yourself and put yourself down. "There I am messing up my life again. I'm hopeless. When will I ever learn?"

This, again, is not taking responsibility for your experience of life. It is important to understand that you have always done the best you possibly could, given the person you were at any particular time. Now that you are learning a new way of thinking, you can begin to perceive things differently and possibly change many of your actions. There is absolutely no need to be upset with your past, present or future behavior. It is all simply part of the learning process – the process of moving yourself from pain to power. And it takes time. You must be patient with yourself. There is *never* any need to be down on yourself. Nothing is your "fault." Yes, you cause your unhappiness, but this is no reason to cast blame. You're simply on the path toward greater self-fulfillment, and it is a lengthy process of trial and error.

3. *Taking responsibility means being aware of where and when you are* NOT *taking responsibility so that you can eventually change.* It took years before I realized that the place I played the victim role most often was with the men in my life. I remember many evenings of complaining for countless hours with my girlfriends about the grief the men in my life were causing me.

Those "jerks," as I so self-righteously called them, were always doing something to take away my happiness. One was always late, one was incredibly stingy, one didn't make enough money, one loved to play golf too much, one wouldn't get a divorce, and so on. I was able to build up incredible anger and resentment about them. Hours and hours on the phone of "Would you believe he actually . . ." Naturally, my loyal friends shared my drama as I shared their upsets about their men. It was a Moan and Groan Society. We never seemed to tire of each other's stories. No wonder: we fed each other the martyrdom we were obviously enjoying, and we always got to be right! The payoff was that we didn't have to create our own happiness – we could simply blame men for not giving it to us.

During this time I was certain I was taking responsibility for my life. Just like my friend Mara, I was making a wonderful living. I had a great apartment. I was totally "independent." But I *wasn't* taking responsibility for my life. I was still expecting the men in my life to "make me happy." I finally learned there is really only one person in the world who can make me happy, and that is ME! Ironically, only through this realization was I able, for the first time, to have a wonderfully nurturing relationship.

Now I know that when I am angry at my husband, I simply have to ask myself, "What am I not doing in my life that I could be doing that I am blaming him for not doing for me?" (Read that one again!) I am now quickly able to tune into what it is. Either I'm being obsessive about money, or I'm feeling insecure, or I'm not creating enough activity for myself, or I'm expecting him to make "all better" something I'm not handling, or whatever.

Once I realize what I am doing, I can get into the task of correcting it. As I correct what needs to be handled in my life, all my anger toward others disappears. My daughter, Leslie, recently commented on how fantastic my marriage is. "Yes," I said, "it's amazing how perfect Mark becomes when I stop expecting him to handle my life!"

This is not to say that you aren't entitled to have your basic needs met by your partner – the need to be supported in your growth, the need to be nurtured at times, the need to know there is caring on your spouse's part – but when you are not handling your life, no amount of caring and nurturing is enough. You become a bottomless pit. The man in your life could stand on his head for you, as some of the men in my life tried to do, but it is never enough.

I might add that if someone is not supplying your basic needs to be nurtured and loved, certainly you would serve yourself by leaving. But first you must ask yourself, "Is it that (s)he is so terrible, or is it simply that I am not taking responsibility for my experience of life?" If you are satisfied that you simply do not choose to spend your life with this person, then it is also taking responsibility to move on with the intention of finding a more compatible partner.

One clue that you are truly taking responsibility is when you feel little or no anger toward this person. You realize that you chose to be there in the past and you are now choosing to leave. Nothing is the other's fault. (S)he is doing the best (s)he can given her (his) level of personal growth. Anger is your clue that you are not taking responsibility.

Relationship with another is only one area where you can give away your power. It is important to look at all other areas of your life as well, to determine where you are not taking responsibility. Your clue will be any one of the following signs:

anger	impatience
upset	joylessness
blaming others	fatigue
pain	attempt to control others
lack of focus	obsessiveness
self-pity	addictions
envy	judgmentalness
helplessness	disappointment
constant state of limbo	jealousy

This is not a complete list, but you get the idea. Whenever you feel any of these, determine what *you* are not doing in your life that is causing the telltale sign. You will be surprised how easy it is to locate where you are abdicating responsibility.

4. *Taking responsibility means handling the Chatterbox.* This is the little voice inside, the voice that tries to drive you crazy – and often succeeds! I'll bet some of you don't even know it's there (I was shocked when I became aware of it), but I promise you it holds the key to all your fears. It's the voice that heralds doom, lack and losing. We're so used to its presence we often don't even notice it is talking to us. If you are not aware of your Chatterbox, it sounds something like this:

If I call him maybe he'll think I'm too pushy, but maybe if I don't call him, he'll think I'm not interested. But if I call him and his message machine is on I'll wonder where he is and it will ruin my whole evening because I'll know he is out with another woman, but if I don't call I'll wonder anyway. Maybe I shouldn't go out tonight. He might call and then he'll think I'm out with someone else and he'll think I don't care. But if I call he'll really know I'm interested and he'll probably start backing away from me. I wonder why he hasn't called. Maybe I was too cool this afternoon when I bumped into him at lunch. Maybe I should have been warmer. I wish I'd been wearing something more attractive. I look so fat in this outfit. And my make-up was terrible. He seemed a little cool. I wonder if it was because he heard I went out with Allen the other night. Well, I don't think he should expect me to sit home every night and wait for him to call. He has a lot of nerve if he expects that. The next time I see him I'll ask him why he hasn't called. We were supposed to go to the movies this week, and he didn't even remember. I'm going to confront him with his lack of responsibility. I won't be judgmental, but I'll certainly let him know how I feel. . . .

Or this:

I'm really angry at my boss for not including me in the meeting this morning. He really doesn't appreciate all the work I do for him. The others spend their day loafing and they get invited to the meeting. Maybe I'll try loafing and see if he likes that better. It really doesn't pay to give your all to a job. You never get rewarded for all the hard work. It just pays to be a big manipulator, like all the rest. An honest hard worker is just not appreciated any more. I'll show him. I'll look around for another job. But the job market is so lousy right now, I'd never find anything. I wish I had completed my master's degree – then I'd have a better chance. I'm really stuck here . . . no one is hiring people

over forty any more. It's all in who you know. If my
parents had had money, I would have been able to
socialize with people who have some clout. I really feel
used. I can't believe they excluded me from the
meeting. Who does he think he is? This kind of thing
always happens to me. . . .

No wonder so many of us hate being alone and can't be
in a room without turning on the radio or television for
company. Anything to escape such insanity! Be assured that
this "insanity" seems to be an unavoidable phase in the
growth process. We are all victims of our Chatterboxes at
some point in our lives.
    Now that you know it exists, you will also notice that you
can't seem to turn it off – at least not yet. The good news is
that there are very effective ways to get rid of this kind of
negativity, which will be discussed in later chapters. For
now, simply notice that your Chatterbox is making you a
victim, and commit yourself to replacing it with a loving
voice. You don't have to hang out with enemies, even if
they are within yourself. By the way, once you get rid of the
negativity your Chatterbox brings, you will really begin to
enjoy being alone.

5. *Taking responsibility means being aware of payoffs that
keep you "stuck."* Payoffs explain why we choose to
perpetuate what we don't want in our lives. Once you
understand payoffs, your behavior will make much more
sense to you. Let me give you a few examples.

Jean
Jean was feeling horribly stuck in her job and wanted
desperately to get out. She viewed herself as a victim. Poor
Jean! Her Chatterbox constantly played the "if only" game.
If only the job market were a little better, she wouldn't have
a problem. If only she had better skills, there would be more

opportunity. What was really keeping Jean at her job? What were the payoffs?

By remaining a victim, Jean had clearly become comfortable. She didn't have to face possible rejection in her search for a new job. Although she hated her job, it was easy. She knew she could handle it; she didn't have to question her competence. She put in her hours and didn't have to expend any additional energy. And the job was relatively secure.

Once Jean became aware of all her payoffs, she had at least three choices. The first was to stay where she was and continue to be miserable. The second was to stay where she was and choose to enjoy her job. The third was to choose to find a more satisfying job.

What did she ultimately do? After recognizing the payoffs for what they were, she was able to break away and find a new job. As long as she was in the victim mode, she was stuck. As soon as she realized she was choosing to stay because of the payoffs, *and not because of her "if only"s,* she was able to move.

Kevin

Kevin had been separated from his wife for five years. Although he had found someone else he wanted to marry, he was not able to tell his wife and children that he wanted a divorce. When the new woman threatened to leave, he sought professional help. The "victim" story his Chatterbox was telling him was that his wife would kill herself, his children would never talk to him again and his parents would disown him. Poor Kevin! He really believed all this on a conscious level and was paralyzed with guilt.

With the help of a therapist, it did not take him long to see that the real problem was his own fear of letting go. Though he no longer loved his wife, she unconsciously represented a psychological "place to come home to," and he was frightened to sever the tie permanently. That was his payoff for staying stuck.

As soon as Kevin was able to see that his own irrational fear was stopping him, he immediately started proceedings to divorce his wife. Naturally, his wife did not kill herself, his children never stopped talking to him, and his parents didn't disown him. They wondered what had taken him so long! The point is that once he recognized that his payoffs were the reason he was choosing to remain in the marriage, his guilt disappeared and he was able to take action.

Tanya

Tanya was always sick, which interfered greatly with many of the things she wanted to do in life. She truly saw herself as a "poor thing" endowed with an unhealthy body. A full-fledged victim if you ever saw one! In one of my workshops, I asked the group to list the payoffs for staying "stuck" in whatever it was that was bothering them. Tanya could find no payoffs for being sick all the time . . . until the group helped her out.

They pointed out to her that her illness got her a lot of attention and that it kept her from having to put herself out there in the world and take any risks. She denied it at first, but finally was able to acknowledge that there was some truth in what they were saying.

Tanya had never looked at her unhealthiness as manipulation, though her unconscious knew exactly what it was doing. As a child, illness was the only device that got her any attention. Tanya's awareness of the payoffs was the impetus she needed to turn her life around. Realizing that she was possibly *creating* her ill health, she made a lot of changes in her life.

First, she completely changed her diet and joined a health club. As important – perhaps more so – she asked the significant others in her life to help her by "rewarding" her only when she was well and ignoring her when she was sick. They obliged after a little practice. She began creating work goals for herself and pushing herself to meet them, even when she was sick. She began doing many of the positive exercises in this book – such as using affirmations and inspirational audios.

When she fully realized her payoffs for being ill, Tanya was able to choose: Did she want to get attention for being sick all her life, or did she want to find a more satisfying way of relating to people and to her life goals? Did she always want to be an observer of life rather than a participant? She chose the latter . . . and sickness is no longer an issue in her life.

From these case studies, you can see the power that hidden payoffs can have in our lives. They are not difficult to discover once you realize they exist. It's simply a matter of sitting down with a pencil and paper and listing them. Sometimes they are obvious to others, but masked from your own vision. If you can't find them, ask a friend to help. You might be surprised to discover that your friends know more about your motives than you do.

6. *Taking responsibility means figuring out what you want in life and acting on it.* Set your goals – then go out and work toward them.

Figure out what kind of space you would like to live in . . . then create it. It doesn't take a lot of money to create a peaceful, loving home for yourself.

Look around and see who you would love to include in your circle of friends . . . then pick up the phone and make plans to get together. Don't sit around waiting for them to call you.

Check out your body. Determine what you need to do to create what looks and feels healthy . . . then make it happen.

Most of us do not "sculpt" our lives. We accept what comes our way . . . then we gripe about it. Many of us spend our lives waiting – waiting for the perfect mate, waiting for the perfect job, waiting for perfect friends to come along. There is no need to wait for anyone to give you anything in your life. You have the power to create what you need. Given commitment, clear goals and action, it's just a matter of time.

7. *Taking responsibility means being aware of the multitude of choices you have in any given situation.*

One of my students put it this way: "From the time my alarm clock rings, I have an hour and a half alone and I realize it's all up to me what the day is going to start like. It's up to me whether I'm going to open the shades and let the light in or mess around in the dark. It's my choice to lie in bed and say 'Yuck, I don't want to get up and go to work. I didn't finish the report I'm supposed to have ready today.' Or it's my choice to lie in bed and give myself positive self-talk and look forward to the coming day. It's my choice to put the music on, dance around the apartment instead of putting on the negativity of the news or listening to my negative Chatterbox. It's up to me whether I'm going to worry about how my body is not in shape or whether I'm going to tell myself I am in the process of creating a great body. The whole day is up to me!"

As you go through each day, it is important to realize that at every moment you are choosing the way you feel. When a difficult situation comes into your life, it is possible to tune in to your mind and say, "Okay, choose." Are you going to make yourself miserable or content? Are you going to visualize scarcity or abundance? Are you going to put yourself down for getting angry with your husband or are you simply going to notice what insecurity you were feeling at the time and discuss it with him? The choice is definitely yours. Pick the one that contributes most to your aliveness and growth.

Here are some other kinds of choices:

Your friend decides not to go with you on the trip you had planned together. You're really angry. . . . OR . . .

You understand she has her reasons, and you find someone else to share the trip, or you go alone and have a ball!

Your husband is an alcoholic. You spend your whole life trying to change him or scold him. . . . OR . . . You attend Al-Anon meetings and learn to change yourself.

Your flu has caused you to miss the big meeting you were scheduled to attend. You are sure this means the end of your whole career. . . . OR . . . You realize you have limitless ways of creating a successful career for yourself.

Your visit to sunny California is filled with torrents of rain. You lament your bad luck for the entire trip. . . . OR . . . You find ways to make it a great vacation anyway.

By now you can really see that the choice is yours. As you continue to read, you will further your ability to place yourself on the up side of any given situation. Keep in mind that this way of thinking doesn't excuse inappropriate behavior on the part of others in your life. It simply allows you to have a more satisfying life. Fully taking responsibility for your experience of life is a long process that requires much practice. I'm still working on it daily after many years . . . and each day my life gets better and better and better. The point is simply to begin. You will start to feel better immediately.

The following six exercises will help you feel noticeably more powerful in the face of your fears:

1. List all the payoffs you get from staying stuck in some aspect of your life. What don't you have to face? What don't you have to do? What comfort do you get? What image do you get to hold on to? Be as honest with yourself as you possibly can. When you are aware of what you are doing, you will automatically discard a lot of your robotlike behavior. You will lead yourself instead of being led.

2. Be aware of all the options you have during the course of a given day. When you are confronted with a difficult situation, sit down and write in a notebook all the possible ways you can act and feel about it. Close your eyes and picture yourself happy about it . . . then sad about it . . . then outrageous . . . then humorous . . . then heavy . . . then light . . . and so on. You will begin to see how easy it is to change your point of view – hence, your feelings. You are in control.

Each time you are upset, be conscious of the alternatives available to you. Again, make it a game. In no way should you put yourself down for being upset. It's a great clue as to where you need to begin taking responsibility.

3. Start noticing what you say in conversations with friends. See if it includes a lot of complaining about other people, such as, "Would you believe that Jill was late for dinner again? We had the biggest fight – right in the restaurant." If this sounds familiar, see if you can turn the situation around so that you learn something new about yourself. For example, "I notice that when Jill is late, I begin to feel really angry. I wonder why I feel that way? I think it's because she doesn't seem to have any respect for my time. On the other hand, part of me likes it. It makes me feel superior always to have something to gripe about. . . ."

4. In a notebook, list the many choices available to you that can change presently upsetting experiences into positive ones. Using the example of Jill's lateness, what choices could you make?

You could stop meeting with her; arrive later, knowing she will be late; bring some interesting reading material;

relax. If meeting on time is essential, you could simply tell her that if she is not there by an agreed-upon hour, you will not wait. There is no reason for anger.

The key is not to blame others for your being upset. This is not to condone the behavior of others, but simply not to allow it to be the source of your upset.

In every situation there are at least thirty ways to change your point of view. Make this another game – the "change your point of view" game. Play it with a friend; having a "growth buddy" is very nourishing.

5. Begin to look at the gifts you have received from what you have always looked at as a "bad" situation. For example, if you are still hurting from your divorce, begin to focus on the good things you had during the marriage and the good things that have come about as a result of the divorce, such as new friends, new ways of dealing with money, freedom, less dependency.

6. This one is really tough! See if you can go one week without criticizing anyone or complaining about anything. You will be surprised how difficult this is. You will also be surprised to learn how much complaining and criticizing you do.

By the way, when you ultimately stop putting down other people in your life, it may seem as if you have nothing left to talk about with your friends. Griping is a habit and needs to be replaced by something more positive. This takes a bit of time and ingenuity, but it will be far more satisfying and joyful.

Seven Ways to Reclaim Your Power

1. Avoid casting blame on an external force for your bad feelings about life. Nothing outside yourself can control your thinking or your actions.

2. Avoid blaming yourself for not being in control. You are doing the best you can and you are on the way to reclaiming your power.

3. Be aware of when and where you are playing the victim role. Learn the clues that tell you that you are not being responsible for what you are being, having, doing or feeling.

4. Familiarize yourself with your biggest enemy – your Chatterbox. Use the exercises throughout this book to replace it with a loving internal friend.

5. Figure out the payoffs that keep you "stuck." Paradoxically, once you find them, you will probably be able quickly to become "unstuck."

6. Determine what you want in life and act on it. Stop waiting for someone to give it to you. You'll be waiting a long time.

7. Be aware of the many choices you have – in both actions and feelings – in any situation that comes your way. Choose the path that contributes to your growth and makes you feel at peace with yourself and others.

5

Pollyanna Rides Again

"**D**on't be such a Pollyanna!"*
How many times has someone tried to put you down with these words when you were trying to look at the brighter side of things? For many years I never questioned that being a Pollyanna was a bad thing. It was unconsciously hammered into my head.

Having dinner with a friend one evening, I fervently tried to make her see the positive side of something she fervently viewed as negative. Suddenly she disdainfully remarked, "You're beginning to sound like Pollyanna." Much to her surprise and mine, I blurted out, "What's so terrible about Pollyanna, anyway? What's wrong with feeling good about life despite the obstacles in your way? What's wrong with looking at the sun instead of seeing gloom and doom? What's wrong with trying to see good in everything? *Nothing* is wrong with it!" I asserted. "In fact," I added incredulously, "why would anyone *resist* thinking that way?"

Pollyanna is a delightful story about a young girl who made a game of finding "something to be glad about" in anything negative that came into her life. Over the years this kind of "Pollyanna" thinking has been maligned as being naive and unrealistic.

And resist we do! Positive thinking is one of the most difficult of all concepts to get across to people. When I present my ideas on positive thinking in my workshops and classes, many of my students respond immediately with "Oh, that's not realistic!" When I question them about what makes negative thinking more realistic, they cannot give me an answer. There is an automatic assumption that negative is realistic and positive is unrealistic. Upon inspection, this is pure madness.

It is reported that over 90% of what we worry about never happens. That means that our negative worries have less than a 10% chance of being correct. If this is so, isn't being positive more realistic than being negative? Think about your own life. I'll wager that most of what you worry about never happens. So are you being realistic when you worry all the time? No!

If you think about it, the important issue is not which is more realistic, but, rather, *Why be miserable when you can be happy?* If being a Pollyanna creates a happier world for you and those around you, why hesitate for one more moment?

Let's look at examples of these two attitudes. Joan and Mary were both housewives in their midforties when their husbands suddenly died. Joan immediately took on the mantle of tragedy. For years, she solicited sympathy from everyone, until it reached the point where no one wanted to be in her company. She then had "proof" that single women never get invited anywhere. She convinced herself that she would never find anyone to love her again, and, naturally, that's what her attitude and behavior were creating for her. Because her husband left her only enough money for survival, she decided she would have to live on that amount, since someone her age would never find a job. She went to a few interviews, but with her lack of enthusiasm, she understandably never landed a job. Her negativity created a "realistic" life of misery.

Mary, on the other hand, took a Pollyanna attitude after her husband's death. Following a short period of mourning, she picked herself up and started all over again. She was one of those individuals who truly believed that one can create good from anything. She too was left without any extra money, and she determined that it was now time to go out and obtain money for herself.

Although Mary had never worked before, she was confident that a place for her existed in the job market. She had always done volunteer fund raising and liked it immensely. On the basis of her experience as a volunteer, she applied to be an assistant in the fund-raising department of a medium-sized charity. Within two years, she found herself totally in charge. Throughout this period she was feeling a sense of expansion and growth she had never felt before. Although she would not have wished her husband's death and still misses him at times, she realizes she has grown enormously as a result of having to make it on her own.

Unlike Joan's friends, Mary's never excluded her from any of their plans. Why would they? She always brought an incredible sense of enthusiasm and exuberance to life. The way she turned her tragedy into triumph served as an inspiration to everyone. Her positive outlook created a very "realistic" life of joy and satisfaction.

Nothing is realistic or unrealistic – there is only what we think about any given situation. *We create our own reality.*

What does this have to do with fear? Everything! Remember, to handle fear is to move from a position of pain to one of power. Although both women had their fears, Joan held hers from a position of pain, whereas Mary held hers from a position of power. Joan's fears resulted in stagnation; Mary's fears resulted in growth.

Joan still worries about not having enough friends, about dying alone, about running out of money. Her heaviness is ominous. She truly lives her life on the left side of the Pain-to-Power Chart – helpless, depressed, paralyzed.

Mary's fears, on the other hand, led to her raising more than enough money for her organization, doing a good job on a television interview, getting a newsletter printed in time, and other successes. Her fears have a totally different quality from Joan's. She lives on the right side of the Pain-to-Power Chart – at ease in her world, excited and motivated. There is absolutely no question that learning to think more positively will pull you closer and closer toward finding your own power.

I learned an amazing way to demonstrate the effectiveness of positive versus negative thinking from Jack Canfield, co-author of the *Chicken Soup for the Soul* series and President of the Self-Esteem Seminars, which I have used in my workshops. I ask someone to come up and stand facing the rest of the class. After making sure the person has no problems with her (or his) arms, I ask my volunteer to make a fist and extend either arm out to the side. I then tell her to resist, with as much strength as she can muster, as I stand facing her and attempt to push her arm down with my outstretched hand. Not once have I succeeded in pushing her arm down on my initial trial.

I then ask her to put her arm down, close her eyes and repeat ten times the negative statement "I am a weak and unworthy person." I tell her really to get into the feel of that statement. When she has repeated the statement ten times, I ask her to open her eyes and extend her arm again exactly as she had before. I remind her to resist as hard as she can. Immediately, I am able to bring down her arm. It is as though all strength has left her.

I wish I could record the expressions on my volunteers' faces when they find it impossible to resist my pressure. A few have made me do it again. "I wasn't ready!" is their plea. Lo and behold, the same thing happens on the second try – the arm goes right down with little resistance. They are dumbfounded.

I then ask the volunteer once again to close her eyes, and

repeat ten times the positive statement "I am a strong and worthy person." Again I tell her to really get into the feeling of the words. Once again I ask her to extend her arm and resist my pressure. To her amazement (and everyone else's) I cannot budge the arm. In fact, it is more steadfast than the first time I tried to push it down.

If I continue interspersing positive with negative, the same results occur. I can push the arm down after the negative statement, I am not able to push it down after the positive statement. By the way – for you skeptics out there – I tried this experiment when I was unaware of what the volunteer was saying. I left the room, and the class decided whether the statement should be negative or positive. It didn't matter. Weak words meant a weak arm. Strong words meant a strong arm.

This is a stunning demonstration of the power of the words we speak. Positive words make us physically strong; negative words make us physically weak. The amazing aspect of this experiment is that it doesn't matter if we *believe* the words or not. The mere uttering of them makes our inner self believe them. It is as though the inner self doesn't know what is true and what is false. It doesn't judge. It only reacts to what it is fed. When the words "I am weak" come in, our inner self instructs the rest of us, "He wants to be weak today." When the words "I am strong" come in, the instruction to your body is "He wants to be strong today."

What does all this tell you? STOP FEEDING YOURSELF NEGATIVE THOUGHTS. Negative thoughts take away your power . . . and thus make you more paralyzed from your fear.

As you know, positive thinking is not a new concept. Aside from Pollyanna, Norman Vincent Peale, Napoleon Hill, Maxwell Maltz, and others popularized the concept many years ago. Their books are still available today. So, why don't people think more *positively?* My guess is that people don't understand what being a positive thinker requires. It takes a special commitment and requires a great deal of practice. And once you get it all down perfectly, a maintenance program is a must. I know of no one who has been able to make "positive" a permanent way of thinking without practice. Such people may exist; I simply haven't met them. In my experience, if you don't practice, you lose the skill. This is the point most people don't seem to understand.

I know it doesn't seem fair that you automatically become negative when you stop practicing the positive. I liken it to exercise. Once you get your body in shape, you can't stop working out. Within a short time your muscles start losing tone, and where you once could do fifty sit-ups, twenty is now your maximum. You must keep at it.

The intellect acts in the same way. When problem solving, stimulating discussion or reading is a part of your daily life, your mind is sharp. After a two-week vacation of lounging on the beach, your brain feels soggy. It takes quite a few days to get your brain back in shape.

Obviously, certain aspects of ourselves need constant reinforcement, and a positive mental attitude is just one of them. To offer some good evidence for this, many years ago I joined a remarkable group called The Inside Edge, founded by Diana and Paul von Welanetz. The group still exists today and is composed of what I consider to be successful and positive people. At each meeting, either one of the group members or an outside speaker gives an inspirational talk that is motivating and energizing. Everyone in the group recognizes the need not only to practice positive thinking, but also to be around positive people.

It is significant that in this group are a number of best-selling authors in the self-help field. They know most of the self-help techniques available, yet they congregate week after week – I might add, at 6:15 in the morning – in order to offer each other support. I would wager that every one of them practices some sort of positive thinking daily. They know that if they miss a day, they feel a little "off."

I know most people resist the fact that constant practice is required, or we would all be positive thinkers. It might help to remember that your shower, your make-up, and your shave also don't last, yet you don't have any resistance to starting your day with showering, shaving or putting on new make-up. These are refreshing activities – and so is positive thinking. In fact, it feels wonderful!

So here you are, a blob of negativity. How do you even begin to turn around those miserable thoughts that take away your power? You begin by doing the same thing you would do if your body were out of shape. You create an exercise program – in this case, to retrain your mind. To do so, *you must take action.*

Before giving you a suggested action plan, I recommend that you have on hand the following to make your daily routine more efficient and certainly more pleasurable:

1. A small audiocassette or CD player, iPod, or all of the above . . . whatever suits you best for "portable" listening.
2. Positive audiotapes and CDs. We are so fortunate in today's world to have such an array of audio material available to us for creating a positive view of life. These include affirmation, relaxation, meditation, motivation, visualization and inspirational audios and CDs. Also, many uplifting books are now available in an audio format. Once you realize the benefits you'll receive from such listening material you will take joy in building an extensive audio library.
3. Positive books that inspire and motivate. I suggest that you buy your books instead of borrowing them from the library. The reason for this is that you will want to underline and write in the books and reread them over and over again. You will want to "own" these books in every sense of the word. They provide an incredible support system that is there for you at all times. You might feel that buying these

books and audios is a costly proposition – and you're right. Yet I can't think of a better investment to help you create a better life. If money is a problem, start slowly. The important thing is: BEGIN!

4. Index cards or Post-it™ Notes.

5. Positive quotes. Find those that really touch you in some way. Some very effective quotes for me are:

> "Ships in harbor are safe, but that's not what ships are built for." – *John Shedd*

> "The best way out is always through." – *Helen Keller*

> "I'm not a failure if I don't make it . . . I'm a success because I tried." – *Unknown*

> "Considering how dangerous everything is, nothing is really very frightening!" – *Gertrude Stein*

And how about:

> "Feel the fear . . . and do it anyway!" – *Susan Jeffers*

Write each quote on an individual index card or Post-it™ Then put them all over the place – on your mirrors, your desk, the refrigerator door, in your car, your diary, and so on. You may want to put one quote that really "speaks" to you on many cards, so that wherever you turn, it's there as a reminder.

If you are artistic, make a decorative poster with your quotes to hang on your wall. Or buy one of those wonderful posters with inspirational sayings on them and use it to decorate your wall.

You will find that your quotes will change often as you move ahead with your life. Different ideas are meaningful at different times. Just keep changing the quotes. Be

creative; try to bring some lightness to the task. As humorist
Jan Marshall said, "Not a shred of evidence exists that life
is serious!" Go overboard and be outrageous until friends
ask you what's going on. Really have fun with this.

6. Affirmations. I mentioned affirmation tapes and CDs
above (#2). What is an affirmation? An affirmation is self-
talk in its highest form. Remember the power of self-talk in
the arm experiment? An affirmation is one of your greatest
tools and the easiest and cheapest to use.

An affirmation is *a positive statement that something is
already happening.* It's not happening tomorrow or in the
future, but right now. Here are a few:

I am breaking through old patterns and moving forward
with my life.
I relax, knowing I can handle it all.
I stand tall and take responsibility for my life.
I know that I count and I act as if I do.
I spread warmth and love everywhere I go.
I let go and I trust it's all happening perfectly.
I peacefully allow my life to unfold.
I am finding the gift in all experiences.
I am powerful and I am loving and I have nothing to fear.
I focus on my many blessings.

These are just a few to get you started. I am such a strong
believer in affirmations that I have created three affirmation
audios: *Inner Talk for a Confident Day, Inner Talk for
Peace of Mind,* and *Inner Talk for a Love that Works.* (See
the Bibliography.) Listening to these audios will certainly
build up your repertoire of affirmations . . . as you build up
your sense of confidence, peace and love.

There are some things to remember about affirmations:

Always state affirmations in the present.
Wrong: I will handle my fears.
Right: I am now handling my fears.

Always phrase affirmations in the positive, rather than
the negative.
Wrong: I am no longer putting myself down.
Right: I am becoming more confident every day.

Select affirmations that feel right to you at any given
time. What feels right changes as your situation and
mood changes.

Now what do you do with all of these tools? I will illustrate
by going through a typical day, putting these positive
thinking tools to use. The whole point of the program can be
summed up in three words: OUTTALK YOUR NEGATIVITY.
And, as you probably already know, this is a challenge.

That internal Chatterbox has incredible staying power. It
will resist in every way it can in order to maintain its power
over you. Once you have that little voice under control,
you've got it made. At that point, positive thinking will
become more automatic, so that just a few daily reminders
will suffice to keep you uplifted. But in the beginning it's
got to be full speed ahead! So let's go through your first day
of outtalking your Chatterbox.

Beginner's Intensive for Positive Thinking

1. As you begin to awaken, turn on your audio machine.
Remember to choose your audio the night before and insert
it in your machine ready for you to press the "ON" button.
An affirmation audio offers you a wonderful way to start the
day (*Inner Talk for a Confident Day* would work beautifully

here). Or you can choose a meditation, motivational or inspirational talk or audio-book as an alternative. What great times we live in for learning and growing! After you press the "ON" button, lie there with your eyes closed and let the powerful and loving thoughts sink in. You have to admit this certainly beats lying there thinking about how you don't want to get up and face all the lousy and scary things you have to do all day.

2. As you get out of bed, pay attention to the positive quotes you've surrounded yourself with – on the wall, the refrigerator, your mirror, and so on. You might want to chuckle a bit at what it takes for the human race to make itself feel good!

3. As you dress, it's a great time to play some music that makes your heart sing. That could be relaxation music, rock music or classical music, or whatever feels right for you at any given moment.

4. Also, as you dress, begin to repeat the affirmations you have chosen for the day. A great place to repeat your affirmations is in front of the mirror. Repeat your affirmations for at least ten minutes and continue throughout the day whenever negativity tries to enter your thinking. It requires vigilance to notice the negativity is there. It sneaks in so quietly. But as soon as you are aware of it, begin replacing this negativity with your affirmations. Don't let the little voice take over. *Outtalk your Chatterbox!* I promise you that with practice the negative voice will be the rarity and the positive voice the norm. Just believe that constant repetition will do the trick eventually.

NOTE: In the beginning, I suggest that you do not turn on the television or radio and listen to the news, if that is your habit. The presentation of the news is overwhelmingly negative. For the time being, let your chosen positive voice be the only news you hear as you prepare for the happenings of the day. If it is your habit to read the newspaper as you eat breakfast, read one of your inspirational or motivational self-help books instead.

While teaching a fear class in New York, as an experiment I instructed my students to stay away from the news entirely. They were surprised at the positive difference it made in their lives. Instead of talking with friends about how miserable the world situation was, they began sharing the positive ideas they learned from the self-help books, and their conversations became more animated and exciting.

Once you've acquired the positive thinking habit, you can resume reading the entire paper and listening to the news. You may find you have developed a more constructive approach to the media, seeing in "bad news" opportunities to begin taking responsibility for yourself and your community.

5. If you exercise daily, that is an opportune time to pump in your positive thinking. Affirmations such as, "I can feel the energy coursing through my body" and "I am creating a beautiful day" will make your exercise routine far more effective.

6. Breakfast is over and it is now time to get yourself to work. I live in Los Angeles and I often hear people lamenting about the time they have to spend in their automobiles. Not me! I have made my car my "temple of learning" and I can't wait to get into it. As soon as I turn on the motor, I turn on one of my tapes or CDs. I listen to either motivational or inspirational messages or stirring music. This is time that some people see as wasted and I see as immensely productive. Without my car trip, I lose out on a lot of listening time.

NOTE: Do not use your relaxation or meditation audios in the car, for obvious reasons.

If you walk to work, modern audio equipment can make listening to your audios along the way possible . . . or you can simply repeat your affirmations over and over again.

If you work in your home, you are in luck, because you can play your positive messages all day as you do your chores and run your errands. And if you have small children at home, think about the positive impact these tapes will have on their young and impressionable minds.

7. As you walk into your office, be aware of the positive messages you have already placed there. Again, chuckle to yourself. It helps you to lighten up about *everything*!

8. Pick one special affirmation for the day. Then write it in your diary. If you are running short of affirmations, choose one that feels right for you from my "Inner Talk" books or audios. Or, you can visit my website and use the daily affirmation that I place there. Every time you refer to your diary, say the affirmation at least 10 times. You can also place a special affirmation on your desk where it is constantly visible. Right now the affirmation on my desk is, "It's all happening perfectly." It is there to remind me that no matter what happens relative to any situation in my life, I will learn and grow from it all. A great reminder, indeed!

9. Unless you are a total masochist, you will want to maintain the high energy and fearless state you plugged into with your early-morning ritual. As daily pressures and doubts begin to seep in, simply give yourself a "fix" of positive energy. All you have to do is repeat your affirmations over and over again until you feel your strength and optimism return. Your Chatterbox will also be trying to enter your consciousness all day; remember to outtalk it. Keep these positive fixes going day and night.

10. Before you go to sleep, put a relaxation tape into your audio machine and let in the soothing messages. *Inner Talk for Peace of Mind* would be a very good choice to send you off to a restful and happy sleep . . . or any other audio that gives you a feeling of peace. This is much better than listening to your Chatterbox, which tries to convince you that your life is lacking and that you are not good enough. Awful! Instead, drift off to blissful sleep with the recording feeding you messages of love and caring.

Please believe me when I tell you that if you commit yourself to such a program your whole world will turn around. Positive thinking changes everything in your life. Without your negative Chatterbox, you will wonder what you were always so afraid of before. You will have energy you never thought possible. You will laugh a lot and love a lot more. You will draw more and more positive people into your life. You will be healthier physically. You will be happy to be alive.

In a short period of time (you'll know when you are ready), you can ease up a bit and begin a maintenance program. Give yourself at least one month, however, before you cut back. If on some days you were not as diligent as you would have liked, *don't* let your Chatterbox scold you. I can just hear it in there saying, "See, you can't even follow a simple program like this. You'll never feel good. You're hopeless." Just keep remembering that it's only your Chatterbox speaking, and you can outtalk it. "I'm doing it all perfectly!" is a wonderful affirmation when the Chatterbox tries to tell you you've goofed.

I can't stress enough that positive thinking needs daily practice. I've been practicing it for years and still spend some time each day focusing on the elimination of negativity from my thinking. If I stop completely, as I have on occasion, I know my good feelings will slowly diminish.

Thank goodness, it is easy to get into the swing of it again simply by following the program. I always ask myself then, "Why do I stop doing something that makes me feel so good?"

One more important thought about positive thinking: It is important that you don't use it as an excuse for denial. We begin to feel so good feeling the power of positive thoughts that it is tempting to stifle the sadness and pain that exists, not only in our own lives, but in the world as well.

Yes, there is pain in our own lives. We all experience loss and disappointment. No one is immune. And real positive thinking allows the tears to flow . . . always knowing we will get to the other side of the pain and live a beautiful and productive life. Yes, there is pain in the world . . . and real positive thinking allows the tears to flow for the world as well. Starvation exists. Racism exists. Threats of war exist. Environmental problems exist. And on it goes. Let the tears flow, and then *get involved!* Approach your involvement with the positive sense that something can be done, even if the answer is not readily seen. Denial creates inactivity . . . and so does hopelessness.

No one is immune to pain, and it shouldn't be denied when it exists. The key is to know that you can lead a productive and meaningful life *no matter what the external circumstances are.* What positive thinking does is offer a power boost to help you handle whatever life gives you. Your "bad breaks" do not dominate your life; your indomitable strength does. And when you feel that indomitable strength, you really can handle any of your fears from a position of power – the kind of power that really can make things happen.

6

When "They" Don't Want
You To Grow

The gloom and the fog are beginning to lift. Life is appearing far more manageable now that you have adopted your "Pollyanna" attitude. As you begin to put your new-found positiveness into action and make some longed-for changes, you suddenly find that something is amiss with the people in your life. Both inside and outside your home, you begin to realize that some of the significant people in your life don't seem to like the changes in you – even if the old you was a total wreck! What is happening?

What is happening is that others have become accustomed to interacting with you in a certain way, and when that pattern of interaction is broken, there is usually upset of varying degrees. Even when you understand it, this upset can be very disturbing. Not only are you fearful of moving forward, you are now fearful of losing your relationships. Just when you are in need of a cheering squad, you find yourself faced with enemy troops!

Before I discuss how to deal with family members who are having a hard time with your growing, take a good hard look at the people in your life generally. Do they support your growing or do they drag you down? Do you feel good being around them or do you feel "contaminated" by their negativity? Are they excited about the new you that is emerging or would they prefer the company of the old you that you are outgrowing? If the latter part of all three questions is true, it is time to consider making some changes.

Keep in mind that your goal is to move yourself from pain to power in the way you hold your fear, and remember this:

**It is amazingly empowering
to have the support of a strong,
motivated and inspirational group
of people.**

If you are now cringing with the realization that the people in your life belong in the weak, stuck and depressed category, don't worry. *Awareness* of this fact is the key to the solution. Most of us are *not* aware that we belong to the moan-and-groan crowd until we stop moaning and groaning. When we become aware, things automatically start to take care of themselves.

How? It's quite simple. As you begin to grow, you will notice you no longer want to be around depressing people. Negativity is contagious, and you walk away feeling lousy after spending time in the company of a negative person. Positiveness is contagious as well, and spending time with a positive person makes you feel as though you can sprout wings and fly. Soon you'll become discerning. Energy is tangible, and as you become more aware, you will "feel" if a person is positive or negative . . . and you'll be automatically drawn to the more positive. The people in your life are a good indicator of where you are operating on an emotional level. Like attracts like. As you begin to change, you will automatically draw and be drawn to a different kind of person.

When this is discussed in my classes, the question that always arises is: "That's all well and good, but what do I do with the old friends I have outgrown?" Many of my students have expressed guilt at the thought of leaving old friends behind. This is understandable, but totally unwarranted. In the first place, they are assuming that their old friends are not strong enough to carry on without them. This is a bit presumptuous and more than a bit belittling to their friends. I can guarantee that as you withdraw from their lives, they will find new friends with whom to associate. The Moan and Groan Society will be around for many years to come, and your friends will always find a welcome home there.

There is another possibility: your new-found energy may awaken your friends to new possibilities, and they may join you on your journey toward power, action and love. That, of course, would be ideal. It is important to remember that, even with your old friends as company, you will want to expand your support system so that you will have all kinds of "advanced" role models to show the way.

What kind of support system am I talking about? The kind that makes you feel *wonderful* about yourself. So that when you say you want to go back to school, or get a new job, or whatever, your friends will say, "I think that is a fantastic idea. You'll do beautifully. Don't worry . . . you have what it takes! Go for it!"

This is the kind of support I'm talking about, instead of: "Aren't you taking a big risk? There's so much competition out there, you'll never make it. Why don't you just leave things the way they are?" When you hear that kind of talk, it's time to run the other way.

Among the new friends you make, include those who are farther along the journey than you are at the moment. As Marilyn Ferguson states in her acclaimed book *The Aquarian Conspiracy:*

If we are to find our way across troubled waters, we are better served by the company of those who have built bridges, who have moved beyond despair and inertia.

Although it is a great feeling to be able to lead people to a better place, it is also a relief to be led by others who can show you the way. Life becomes more fun and less of a struggle when you don't have to pioneer on your own. There is a lightness about positive people. They have learned not to take themselves so seriously and they are a joy to be around. This is not to say that positive thinkers are "flaky." The Inside Edge, the group I mentioned in the last chapter, not only supports positive thinking but also supports people in expanding their own vision into the world to create a healthier planet. When we are concerned with something bigger than ourselves, our fears are greatly diminished. We sense ourselves as being part of a bigger whole – we are not alone and we, perhaps for the first time, are aware of a sense of purpose.

It is incredibly important to your peace of mind and sense of power to have some kind of support group. I can't stress enough how important it is to begin *now* to have strong people in your life, in the form of an established group or simply a group of friends who are consciously in the process of growing. Again, don't worry about your negative friends. It is more than likely that as soon as you stop agreeing with their victim act, they will either disappear or join you on the path to power and love.

How do you begin? Think about people you have recently met and really admire. Do some sleuthing to find out their telephone numbers. Call them up and tell them simply that you were impressed at the first meeting and that you would like to get to know them better. Then invite them to join you for lunch or dinner. I know this can be *very* frightening at first. The first time I did it, many years ago, my "hand' actually shook as I dialed the phone.

Much to my surprise, the woman I had chosen for my first new friend was thrilled that I had called. At that time my self-esteem was so low, I imagined she would do everything to avoid me. On the contrary, she told me she was really excited I had called, "You are?" was my insecure response. We had a delightful evening together, and continue to be good friends today. Initiating relationships became easier for me as time went on, and today I'm blessed with a circle of fantastic friends.

The point is that you must make the effort. So many people sit at home waiting for the phone to ring and wondering why they are always alone. Nothing is going to come to you – especially in the beginning. You have to go out and create the kind of support system you want. Even if it seems frightening, *do it anyway*! Even if you get a few rejections, keep dialing. If you get one good response out of ten, that's great. Remember that people are flattered by your interest, even if for their own reasons they reject your invitation. You will have made them feel good simply by calling. Be discriminating in who you call. Pick someone you perceive as being a few steps ahead of you in personal growth. It will be great for your self-confidence when you eventually find out that you're way ahead of them in many areas. We do tend to greatly underestimate ourselves.

A good place to find such people is at self-improvement classes, workshops or seminars. There you will meet people already on the path of personal growth. You will have much in common, and the likelihood is that you will find more openness with such people.

Now that you've got your friends in order, your next question might be: *"What do I do when my mate is the one who is dragging me down?"*

This is an important question. It is often our mate who resists our growth most of all. Although we are often shocked and disappointed at his or her lack of support, it isn't really so surprising. Our mates often perceive that they have much to lose when we begin rocking the boat. It might take a while for them to realize they have more to gain by our growth. The following two stories are extreme examples of how difficult it is for a mate to accept change – even if that change is from sickness to health.

Doris

Doris was one of my earliest students. She lived in Garden City, Long Island, and for eighteen years had been too frightened to venture any farther. In fact, during the few years prior to her attending my class, she had hardly left her home. She was, as you might have guessed, an agoraphobic. My teaching is geared toward everyday fears, as opposed to phobias. Yet something drew her to my course.

In order for her to get there, her husband, Ted, had to drive her into New York, take her up to the classroom and wait for her downstairs. She was too frightened to be on her own. When it was her turn to speak in the go-around, I could see the anguish on her face. She was panicked that she was going to have a panic attack.

I used the technique called "paradoxical intention" on Doris, which, simply stated, was to encourage her to do the very thing she feared. What we resist, persists. So I told her *not* to resist and to show us what a panic attack looked like. As predicted, she couldn't muster one up no matter how hard she tried, and ultimately she began to laugh, as did the rest of us. From that moment, she was on her way back to health. She was diligent about doing all the homework assignments, and within a short time she was driving, shopping, and even taking the subway. The class and I watched her transform before our eyes.

One day she came into class a bit disturbed. She said, "As I begin to feel better and better, I'm realizing that my husband is trying to sabotage me. Every time I leave the house, he tries to put all kinds of fear thoughts into my head. When I come home excited about some new thing I've conquered, he withdraws and becomes very aloof. I'm so angry at him! I don't understand what is happening! Why would he do that to me?"

To all of us who have dramatically changed our patterns of relating to people in our lives, the answer was obvious. Ted was doing it for a number of reasons. In the first place, he was threatened by her changes. Before she took the path to recovery, he had a wife who was always waiting for him at home. He never had to concern himself with suspicions of what she might be doing in the outside world. There was a tremendous security in that, even though their life was so limited as a result of her phobias.

Second, there was probably actual worry connected with his behavior. For years, she was a little bird in a cage. It was doubtful that any harm would come to her in the confines of their home, but now that she was out in the world, traveling the streets of New York, he was undoubtedly afraid that some harm would come to her. As we worry about our children crossing the street alone for the first time, he worried about his "child," who in many ways was crossing the street for the first time.

Last, her independence was worrying him. For so many years she had desperately needed him to function for her. Now she was functioning on her own. Would she continue to want him if the need was no longer there?

With these thoughts going through Ted's head, no wonder he found it difficult to support Doris in her growth. As we talked about what he might be feeling, she began to realize that it was *he* who needed the support from her. She admitted that her anger made it hard for her to give him any support. As she put it, "How do you reassure someone you feel like punching in the face!"

It took a while, but, happily for Doris and Ted, they were able to work through the changes that had to take place in order for the marriage to work on a healthier basis. What helped was the fact that Doris was sure that she would *never* go back to being the pathetic "shut-in" she used to be. If it cost her her husband, so be it! She felt entitled to health after all those years of suffering. It was, therefore, clear to Ted that his manipulations would not work. Either he adjusted or he would lose his wife. His ego was strong enough to overcome his feeling of threat and ultimately he became a tremendous support to Doris.

Rona

The story of Rona and Bill is similar. Rona is now a beautiful woman who looks like she stepped out of a fashion magazine. Three years ago, she weighed 250 pounds. Her doctor warned her that if she did not lose weight, her health would be seriously impaired. With incredible will, she lost the weight and has maintained her slender figure. With the weight loss, a new woman has emerged.

As with Doris, Rona's relationship with her husband went through many changes before he could accept the fact that he had a beautiful wife who attracted the attention of men wherever she went. Subtly, he tried to undermine his beautiful new wife by accusing her of flirting, denying her sex, buying her fattening food, and using other such devices.

Bill is basically a kind man, so he was shocked when he realized he felt threatened by the fact that his wife was becoming healthier. When he saw how destructive his insecurity was to himself and to Rona, he went for professional help. The marriage is now thriving.

Not all relationships are as healthy as those of Doris and Rona, and change in the unwritten contract of the partnership can signal the end of the relationship. Although the thought that your relationship could break down may be very frightening, in actuality I know of *no one* who has chosen the path of growth over his or her relationship who has regretted that choice!

Here are two examples:

Richard

Richard had usually played it safe. He was an accountant who received a biweekly paycheck that supported him, his wife and their two children. In his late thirties, he decided there had to be more to life than he was experiencing. One of the companies for which he had done a great deal of work was available for purchase. It was a small computer company that showed a great deal of promise. When he discussed the idea of raising the capital and buying the company, his wife couldn't deal with it – her financial security was threatened. Obviously, she had no confidence in his ability to make it work.

Richard decided that for his own mental health, he had to give it a try. He might fail, but if he didn't go ahead with it, he would spend the rest of his life doing what he didn't want to do. Despite his wife's disapproval, he made the purchase when he was finally able to raise the capital.

His home situation changed drastically during the process. Naturally, the initial stages of running a new business require a great deal of time. He experienced nothing but resentment on the part of his wife. He got no support or encouragement from her. He asked her to become involved with him in the company, since their children were both able to take care of themselves. She refused.

Their home became a battleground, and when he found himself happy to leave in the morning and unhappy to come home in the evening, he decided it was time to end the relationship. To this day, his wife still considers him to be selfish and uncaring, simply because he wouldn't play the game according to her rules.

Richard ultimately got a divorce and made a marvelous success of the business. He grew, and his wife was not able to grow with him. He shudders when he looks back at where he would still be had he not taken the opportunity that presented itself. His sense of himself has dramatically altered for the better. He felt the fear . . . and did it anyway, even though it meant the breakup of his marriage. He is now remarried, to a woman who encourages his growth as he encourages hers. They are growing together.

Sheila

Sheila also chose growth over an unhealthy relationship. She was married very young and had two daughters in the first four years of her marriage. It did not take long for dissatisfaction to set in, and, with the support of her husband, Roger, she went back to school to complete her education. While initially she was afraid that she had lost her ability to learn after an absence of five years, she was the star in her class and graduated magna cum laude. This success encouraged her to get her master's degree and ultimately her doctorate.

As long as she was a student, things seemed to go well with Roger. He was proud of his "little student" and he really was a marvelous help with the children. When she finally hung her doctoral diploma on the wall, after many years, her relationship with her husband seemed to change. She was no longer his little student. She was a full-fledged professional with an advanced degree – more advanced than his master's degree. At this point the put-downs began, and the lack of communication, and his lateness in coming home from work. He began an affair with another woman, who, not surprisingly, had never gone to college.

Roger was not able to handle Sheila's tremendous growth as a human being, and she ended the relationship. It was painful in the beginning – they had been together twelve years – but she began to experience the joy of discovering her own capabilities. She has never regretted her choice to go back to school and create a thriving career.

Her daughters, upset in the beginning, are now very proud of her enormous success. She serves as an excellent role model for them. She is now married to a man who absolutely adores the fact she is "out there" doing so well.

Her aliveness brightens their life, and he loves her for being such an interesting person. He obviously does not feel threatened by her continuing growth.

I know your relationship with your mate is not something to be taken lightly, and it often takes a tremendous amount of courage to risk rocking the boat. It is always a risk, but one I believe to be worth taking. When you choose to remain "stuck" simply because you don't want to upset your mate, you become resentful of the fact that you have not had your chance to grow. Ultimately, the relationship becomes very strained, and it is not unusual for its breakdown to occur anyway.

My suggestion is:

**Believe that your mate wants what
is best for you and that he or she
will ultimately love the positive changes in you.**

Most probably, your mate will be relieved by your new-found power – it takes some of the responsibility off him or her. Most of us would like to know that the people in our lives are strong and healthy and loving, instead of needy, weak and helpless. Consider this: If your mate turns out to be someone who really prefers you to be needy, weak and helpless, do you really want to be there?

Not only mates have a difficult time when we become alive with possibility. Other family members do, too. Children may become pouty, and parents may become judgmental. They, too, may have become accustomed to relating to us in a certain way, and resist our changing.

The masters of manipulation are children, and believe me when I tell you they will often prey upon tendencies toward guilt. Parents have their own style. Usually their put-downs are subtle and "sweet," such as, "Darling, are you sure you can do it? You've never been much good at doing things on your own, you know?" or "Darling, you'd better rethink getting a divorce. Nobody wants a woman over thirty, especially with two kids" or "You're acting so selfish lately, I hardly recognize you."

Very often parents don't realize they are undermining their children's confidence in themselves, and when this is pointed out to them, they stop the criticism. I once told my mother she obviously had no confidence in me, because she worried about me all the time. She said that was ridiculous, she thought I was the smartest, most competent woman she knew. I pointed out that if that was the case, her worry was unjustified. She looked surprised, and for the first time realized that the way she habitually spoke to me was a carry-over from when I was two, and was not based on today's reality. From this conversation a miracle happened: She became one of my biggest confidence builders. "You can do it. You can do anything you set your mind to do!" Yes, that's really the way she began speaking to me.

Some may be blessed with a family that is supportive in anything they do, but this is not always the case. Often a great deal of possessiveness is felt by family members, and with that comes a tremendous amount of manipulation. It is important that we learn techniques to create a win-win situation for all parties concerned. This is easier said than done. Behavior change is difficult enough without having to deal with the "crazy" behavior of the people closest to us.

Again I speak from experience. When I went back to college, it seemed that everyone was upset – my mother, my then-husband, my children and my friends. My mother couldn't understand how I could "leave" my children; my husband resented the fact that I had a life apart from him; my children laid a guilt trip on me when I wasn't there to administer to their every need; and my friends, who were then all housewives and mothers, sided with all of the above!

To say that this made me feel insecure about my decision would be an understatement. My reaction was to lash out at anyone who was giving me any difficulty. It was a period of great turmoil. At the time, I was not mature enough to understand why they were upset and to react appropriately. In fact, my inappropriateness was supercharged. I was often really obnoxious. I was acting out what I have subsequently called the PENDULUM SYNDROME, which is illustrated below.

As we strive for healthy assertiveness in life, we overshoot the mark in the beginning and swing from Passivity to Aggression many times before we settle into Healthy Assertiveness. More accurately, this swing could be called the PASSIVE-TO-OBNOXIOUS-TO-HEALTHY SYNDROME.

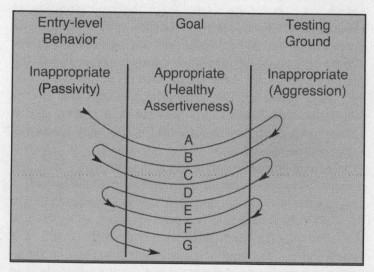

The obnoxious stage can be recognized in the following statements, which are rather mild versions of what came out of my mouth when I was in the throes of the Pendulum Syndrome:

"How dare you!"
"I don't give a damn what you think. I'm doing whatever I please!"
"I don't need you. I never did!"
"You're calling *me* selfish? What about you?"

Although most of us don't like ourselves when we lash out in such a manner, doing it somehow feels better than reverting to the passive "wimp" we used to be. It is often an understandable part of the process of change. We are not yet sure of ourselves and our reaction is to defend with all our might.

This swing to Aggression occurs as we hang on to our new behavior for dear life, afraid of reverting to Passivity once again. Yet every once in a while we get scared and do swing back again to a safe place. Hence, the pendulum swings back and forth as we learn the new language of Healthy Assertiveness. We go from Passivity to Aggression many times before we settle into an appropriate range. Ultimately, we do become more comfortable in expressing our needs and doing what we have to do in this world and we settle down in the appropriate range. But in the beginning, this Pendulum Syndrome is a reality, and it causes much confusion and discomfort, not only for us, but for everyone around us.

Although our behavior is often inappropriate, it is important not to punish ourselves for it. Interestingly, we allow children the leeway they need to test new ways of relating to the world, yet we are hard on ourselves when going through the same process. In reality, we go through fearful new behavioral stages throughout our entire lives, and as we do we are constantly floundering around, until we learn how to do it right.

Again, AWARENESS is the key. Know that in all likelihood, as you start to take risks and grow, you are going to get resistance from people in your life. It's a given. If it isn't your mate, it will be your parents or your children or your friends. When you rock the boat, someone will tell you to sit down. You need not feel shocked, surprised or self-righteous. It is their way of defending their security. Often they don't even know they are doing it. In their minds, these admonitions and observations seem totally justified and "for your own good." What is important is that *you* know what is happening.

It will also help if you acknowledge others when they are supporting you. Let them feel good when they are acting in a nurturing way. Send them a loving note expressing your appreciation or some flowers or balloons or whatever will make them happy. This will reinforce the kind of reactions from them you are seeking and will help *you* focus on their contribution rather than their negativity.

Your awareness of the Pendulum Syndrome should enable you to by-pass some of the swings and handle put-downs more appropriately. There are win-win ways of stopping negative feedback from others. You can learn to respond to significant others in a way that does not demolish them. Here are some examples:

Mom: "You'll never make it out there on your own."

Lose-Lose: "Mind your own business. I'll do as I please!"

Win-Win: "Thank you for your concern, Mom, but I have so much faith in myself, I know that whatever comes up, I'll handle it. I'd like you to have more faith in me too. It would really help me a lot."

The Win-Win answer is clear. It states your confidence in yourself (act-as-if, even if you're not quite sure you *will* make it on your own) and lets her know what you would like from her.

Husband: "Look at yourself. You've become so selfish since you started that job. Do you really like yourself that way?"

Lose-Lose: "You call *me* selfish. Who do you think has been picking up after you all these years? Now it's *my* turn."

Win-Win: "I can see why you think I'm being selfish – I'm not available to you as much as I used to be. All this change is difficult for me as well, but I need to do this for my own growth. If I don't, I know I will hold an awful lot of resentment toward myself and toward you. I really would like to have your support. I know you're feeling a little neglected right now, and it's only natural. I want you to know that I love you very much. What can we do to improve the situation?"

Children: "You don't care about us any more."
Lose-Lose: "You kids have absolutely no appreciation. I've been your slave ever since you were born. Now I do something for myself, and you're complaining!"
Win-Win: "I know it feels different because I'm not around all the time. But I really trust that you guys will find a way to be without me for these few hours. Parents are people too. And it's important for my peace of mind to be able to work."

The dialogue will not always end there, but that is the tenor of a win-win interaction. An excellent book on the subject of non-aggressive self-defense is *Aikido in Everyday Life* by Terry Dobson and Victor Miller. Their premise is that "the best victory is the one in which everyone wins." It describes a gentle way to win and gives many sample dialogues and reasons why they work.

I suggest you also learn some centering techniques, so that when you feel yourself swing over to one extreme or the other you can bring yourself back to a place of balance and harmony. Also relaxation audios, meditation and positive affirmations as described in the last chapter, are a few ways to get yourself to a more peaceful place. Later chapters will offer more tools to gain self-control, so you can have what you want without hurting someone else in the process.

It will greatly help your understanding to know that one of the reasons we react so hostilely when others don't support us is our *need for approval.* Whenever we get upset at the comments of loved ones, it is a clue we are still acting like a child. Guilt is another clue. Guilt and hostility often mask our anger at ourselves and others for our not being able to break unhealthy ties with loved ones. The lashing-out part of the Pendulum Syndrome comes from this unhealthy attachment.

As you become clearer and more adult about what you need to do in order to grow, loved ones will be able to say anything they please and you won't be affected. You can simply give them a big kiss and say, "I love you but I have to live my own life." End of story. No moans and groans. No hysteria about how badly they are all treating you. In a sense, your need to please shows you what you have to work on – and that is: letting go emotionally of the role of child and stepping into the role of adult. As difficult as it is, cutting childlike relationships with others and substituting more responsible ones allow you to act much more lovingly toward other people in your life. It is a paradox. *The less you need someone's approval, the more you are able to love them.*

Look at people in your life as "practice." The way you react to them allows you to see what you have to work on within yourself. Through them you can practice letting go of inappropriate reactions and developing more responsible ways of behaving. So, instead of wanting to throttle your loved ones when they give you a hard time, it is better to look at them as mirrors of what you still need to work on in terms of your personal growth.

If you cannot reason with loved ones about their destructive behavior toward you, it is best to create some distance until you learn to operate on a more adult level. The father of one of my students, Charlotte, actually used to tell her point-blank that, without a doubt, she was incompetent. No beating around the bush on his part! Eventually, she was able to say to him, "You know, Dad, I love you very much, and until you start respecting who I am, I am going to stay away from you. Right now I need people to support me and love me, and that's not what I feel coming from you." She stayed away from him, making only perfunctory holiday calls, until she felt enough inner strength to handle his put-downs. This was not easy. Saying good-bye to the old relationship with a parent usually requires that we go through grief until the old door is closed and the new one is opened. We are, in effect, grieving for the end of an era. The emerging era, however, brings much more satisfaction with it. Much to Charlotte's surprise, when she finally reconnected with her father, the put-downs stopped.

In all likelihood, prior to her new-found growth, she did present to her father a full-blown picture of incompetence. When that changed, so did his reaction to her. Usually inner strength is respected – we get back what we put out.

The most important thing is for you to be your own best friend. Whatever you are doing – don't put yourself down. Slowly begin to discover which, for you, is the path of the heart. Which path in life will make you grow? That is the path to take. You might be surprised when your loved ones ultimately come to understand and respect that. If not, your new strength will allow you to break unhealthy ties and establish new, healthier ones.

7

How to Make a
No-Lose Decision

One of the biggest fears that keeps us from moving ahead with our lives is our difficulty in making decisions. As one of my students lamented, "Sometimes I feel like the proverbial donkey between two bales of hay – unable to decide which one I want, and, in the meantime, starving to death." The irony, of course, is that by not choosing, we *are* choosing – to starve. We are choosing to deprive ourselves of what makes life a delicious feast.

The problem is that we have been taught "Be careful! You might make the wrong decision!" A *wrong* decision! Just the sound of that can bring terror to our hearts. We are afraid that the wrong decision will deprive us of something – money, friends, lovers, status or whatever the *right* decision is supposed to bring us.

Closely tied to this is our panic over making mistakes. For some reason we feel we should be perfect, and forget that we *learn* through our mistakes. Our need to be perfect and our need to control the outcome of events work together to keep us petrified when we think about making a change or attempting a new challenge.

If the above describes you, I am going to demonstrate that

you are worrying needlessly. There really is nothing to lose, only something to gain, whatever the choices you make or actions you take in life. As I stated earlier, *all you have to do to change your world is change the way you think about it.* This concept works beautifully here. You can actually shift your thinking in such a way as to make a wrong decision or mistake an *impossibility*. Let's begin with decision making.

Suppose you are at a Choice Point in life. If you are like most of us, you have been taught to use the No-Win Model as you think about the decision to be made. The model looks like this:

Your heart feels heavy about the choice you have to make.

NO-WIN MODEL

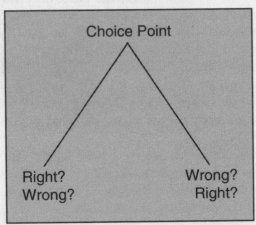

You feel somewhat paralyzed as you think about the consequences in life-and-death terms. You stand at the threshold of the decision, lamenting and obsessing: "Should I do this or should I do that? What if I go this way and that happens? What if it doesn't work out the way I plan? What if . . ." The "what ifs" are out in full force. The internal Chatterbox is at it again. You look at the unknown and try to predict the future; you try to take control of outside forces. Both are impossible. At this point you might notice you are driving yourself crazy.

After the decision is made, the No-Win Model makes you constantly reassess the situation, hoping you didn't make a mistake. You keep looking back and berating yourself with "If only I had . . ." You waste valuable energy and you also make yourself miserable.

You gain relief if the outcome is as you hoped it would be – *but* only temporarily. As you breathe a sigh of relief, you are already worrying that the situation might reverse itself and that it might *ultimately* prove to be the wrong decision. Furthermore, you are already fearful about the next decision you have to make, because you will have to go through the whole agonizing process once again. Look familiar? Crazy, isn't it! Clearly, this is a no-win situation. But there is another way – the No-Lose Model.

Go back and stand at the Choice Point again. This time, the situation looks like this:

NO-LOSE MODEL

Choice Point

"Goodies"   "Goodies"

Path A   Path B
Right!   Right!

Notice that what lies ahead are simply two paths – A and B
– *both of which are right!* Each path has nothing but
"goodies" along the way. You are clearly facing a no-lose
situation. And what are these goodies? They are opportunities to experience life in a new way, to learn and grow,
to find out who you are and who you would really like to be
and what you would like to do in this life. Each path is
strewn with opportunities – *despite the outcome.* "What?
Despite the outcome?" Up to this point you may have been
willing to go along with me, but those three words are
making you a little dubious, if not downright resistant.
"What if . . ." comes up again in your thinking. Let me
answer your "what ifs" with an example.

Imagine you are faced with the choice of staying with
your present job or taking a new one that has opened up for
you. If you stand at the No-Win Choice Point, your
Chatterbox takes over and craziness begins:

"If I stay here I might be missing a very good chance to
move ahead. But if I go, maybe I won't be able to handle my
new responsibilities. What if I get fired on the new job, and
then I have nothing? I really like it here. I'll have more
opportunity to move ahead on the new job. Maybe they'll
promote me and I'll be making more money. But what if I
regret leaving? What if . . . ? Oh, I don't know what to do!
I could ruin my whole life if I make the wrong decision!"

If you stand at the No-Lose Choice Point, your "fearless"
self takes over:

"Isn't it fantastic! I've been offered a new job. If I take it,
I'll have an opportunity to meet new people, to learn new
ways of doing things, to experience an entirely different
work atmosphere and to broaden my base of experience. If
something happens and it doesn't work out, I know I'll
handle it. Even though the job market is difficult right now,

I know somehow I'll find another job if I need one. Even that will be an interesting experience, since I'll learn to deal with the loss of a job and learn to solve the problems that might come up if I am unemployed. If I stay, I have an opportunity to deepen the contacts I have made here. I really feel better about myself having been offered the other job, so if I stay, perhaps I'll ask for a promotion. If for some reason it doesn't work out here, there will be other opportunities to pursue. It's all an adventure, no matter which way I turn."

I really do know people who think this way – and their approach to life is a joy to be around. They truly live in a no-lose world.

Alex is a perfect example. Now a practicing psychologist in Los Angeles, he originally intended to follow in his father's footsteps and become a lawyer. His college grades were excellent, and he had no trouble getting into what was considered a fine law school. He studied hard and did very well the first two years. But the time spent away from home began making a difference in his personal priorities. He came to realize that he didn't want to spend the rest of his life in the "combat zone," as he called it, that being a lawyer required. He wanted to help people in a different way, and he decided that clinical psychology was much more in line with his personality. He also realized that part of his decision to be a lawyer was his desire to please his father. But now he was much more in touch with the person inside himself, and he made the decision to leave law school and pursue a career in psychology. His father gave him his blessing but refused to pay any more of his college expenses, thus increasing the difficulty of the decision. But Alex trusted his gut and withdrew from a situation that did not suit his needs.

Some, including his father, saw those two years at law school as a waste of time, but Alex never saw it that way.

By trying it out, he discovered that being a lawyer was not for him. Finding out what you *don't* like is, paradoxically, as valuable as finding out what you do like. Also, while at law school he made a number of good friends who remain his friends today. And the information he gathered from those first two years has helped him in many personal and professional situations since.

For Alex, the goodies didn't end there. Since his father had stopped paying his expenses, he had to work for two years to obtain enough money to get started on his degree in psychology. Were those two years wasted? Not at all. His job with a construction company was doubly enriching: he was exposed to a different way of life, and, through one of his co-workers, he met the woman who became his wife. Finally, with a fellowship and his two part-time jobs, Alex was able to complete his doctorate.

This set of events was invaluable in terms of teaching Alex to take responsibility for his own life. Perhaps neither he nor his father realized it at the time, but his father really did him a favor by making him stand on his own two feet. Alex learned that if you want something badly enough, there is a way to get it. And if there was a way, he would find it. He knew that if he hadn't been able to obtain a fellowship, he would have found another way. As a result, he approached future decisions with a feeling of power, energy and excitement. Remember that underlying all our fears is *a lack of trust in ourselves.* Each step that Alex took, *despite the outcome,* even when it meant loss of financial support and delay in his education, was an opportunity for him to learn to trust himself to provide for his own needs.

It's interesting to me that when I present the No-Lose Model to my students, the resistance is initially very high. "Oh, come on, you're not being realistic." As I said earlier, we have been taught to believe that negative equals realistic and positive equals unrealistic. When I challenge my students, they can't find more credence in the No-Win Model than in the No-Lose Model, yet the latter can move us from a position of pain to one of power, which is ultimately our goal as we learn to deal with fear. Another point to consider is that *it feels better to come from a no-lose position.* Why continue to resist coming from a no-lose position? Why continue to feel pain, paralysis and depression? Yet we continue to do it until we incorporate into our being another way of seeing the world. Then we can slowly begin to change the no-win thinking that has kept us victimized.

A critical factor in your accepting the No-Lose Model is the way you think about outcomes and opportunities. It might be hard for you to accept the fact that losing a job is a no-lose situation. Traditionally, opportunities in life are thought of as relating to money, status and the visible signs of "success." I'm asking you to think of opportunity in an entirely different light. The purpose of this book is to help you handle fear in a way that allows you to fulfill your goals in life. Every time you encounter something that forces you to "handle it," your self-esteem is raised considerably. You learn to trust that you will survive, no matter what happens. And in this way your fears are diminished immeasurably.

**The knowledge that you can handle anything
that comes your way is the key to allowing yourself
to take healthy, life-affirming risks.**

Getting back to my earlier example, if the outcome of your choosing to move to a new job is for you to lose that job within a few months, you now see how you will have the opportunity to strengthen your self-esteem by facing the storm, regrouping your inner forces, reaching out once again to find a new, perhaps more satisfying, position. In the meantime, you will be meeting new people and enlarging your world. Seen in this light, losing your job becomes a no-lose situation.

I have often said to my students that perhaps the "lucky" ones in life are those who have been forced to face things in their lives that we all hope we will never have to face – things such as losing a job, the death of a loved one, divorce, bankruptcy, illness. Once you have handled any of those things, you emerge a much stronger person. I know of few people who have experienced loss and haven't felt a large measure of pride in themselves at finding a way to make their lives work despite their adversity. They have discovered that *security is not having things; it's handling things*. Thus, when you can answer all your "what ifs" with "I can handle it," you can approach all things with a no-lose guarantee, and the fear disappears.

Now that you've learned there really are no right or wrong decisions when using the No-Lose Model, there are steps you can take to heighten your awareness about the alternatives that lie before you. This awareness will better improve the chances of the outcome being aligned with your wishes, and will give you greater peace of mind. I suggest that the following steps be taken when you face a major decision and after you've made one.

Before Making a Decision

1. *Focus immediately on the No-Lose Model.* Affirm to yourself, "I can't lose – regardless of the outcome of the decision I make. The world is a place for opportunity, and I look forward to the opportunities for learning and growing that either pathway gives me." Push out thoughts of what you can lose and allow only thoughts of what can be gained. Use the exercises in the chapter on positive thinking.

2. *Do your homework.* There is much to learn about the alternatives that lie before you. It is most helpful to talk to as many people as will listen. Don't be afraid to approach professionals relative to the decision to be made. A few might put you off, but most will be happy to help. In fact, they will be flattered that you came to them for advice.

Look for feedback from other sources as well. Talk to people at dinner parties, in the barbershop or beauty salon, the doctor's office, or wherever. People you meet in unlikely places can create a valuable connection for you in ways you never could have imagined, or they might give you an insight learned from their personal experiences.

It is important that you talk to the "right" people. Let me give you my definition of the right people. They are those who support your learning and growing. If you talk to people who constantly put down the possibilities open to you, they are the wrong people to talk to. Politely say thank you and go on to someone else.

One wonderful teacher of mine helped me greatly when he taught me the phrase "First time, shame on you. Second time, shame on me." Applied to this situation, if you discuss something with people who are insensitive to your needs, shame on them. If you continue to allow yourself to be battered by their words, shame on you. You don't have to continue having conversations about your decision with those who make you feel bad about yourself. You should talk to people who can support you with statements like "I think it's terrific you're considering . . ." or "I think you'll do beautifully at . . ." You get the picture. Why put yourself in a position to feel miserable when it's so easy to feel great?

Also, don't hesitate to talk about your plans just because you are fearful that if they don't work out you'll look like a "failure." Swallow your pride. By not investigating as fully as you can, you are cutting off valuable sources of information that might help you enormously. Remember:

**You're not a failure if you don't make it;
you're a success because you try.**

One of my students was concerned about being called a "talker" rather than a "doer" if she made too many false starts. There is no such thing as a false start if you are seriously committed to advancement. My first experience in the publishing world serves as a good example.

Years ago, I made the decision to publish a book of poems I had written. Since I knew nothing about the publishing world, I started talking to as many people as I could about how I should best proceed. I took a course on getting published; I called strangers who worked in various publishing houses (and was surprised that they were most anxious to help); I submitted my book to about twenty publishers, and received one rejection after another. But I just kept talking about my career as a writer. I'm sure there were those who said, "Who's she kidding? It will never happen." Over lunch one day, Ellen Carr, a business associate and now a dear friend, and I decided to write and self-publish a short guidebook for women about getting a job. We were concerned about the number of talented women we knew whose fears of rejection and failure kept them from even trying to enter the job market. Again I started talking about our project to everyone I knew and again a whole series of delays occurred that made some people doubt that the book would ever be published. But I just kept talking, as did Ellen, and we found ourselves meeting all sorts of interesting people who were invaluable in helping us with our project. And that joyous day did arrive when our books were finally delivered to us.

It could be said that there were many false starts in my writing career. Not so! Each step along the way made me more and more ready to enter the field, even though the outcome may not have been in the form originally pictured. And I certainly learned how to deal with rejection! Putting your ideas out into the world by constantly talking about them may create a few doubting Thomases, yet not only does talking bring valuable information, *it clarifies your intention to have it happen!* Intention is a powerful tool in creating something you want in your life.

3. *Establish your priorities.* This will require some soul-searching. Give yourself time really to think about what you want out of life. This is a very difficult thing to discover for most of us, since we are trained at an early age to do what other people want us to do. We are out of touch with those things that really bring us satisfaction. To make it easier, ask yourself which pathway is more in line with your overall goals in life – at the present time.

It is important to remember that goals constantly change as you go through life, and you have to keep reassessing them. The decision you make today might not be the decision you would make five years from now. If you are having trouble clarifying your overall goals, don't worry about it. It may take many more decisions and much more experimentation with different situations to discover how best to order your priorities. At least you are beginning to pay attention to who you are. Allow yourself confusion in the searching process. It is through confusion that you finally come to clarity.

4. *Trust your impulses.* Although you might have difficulty getting to the "person within" through the soul-searching process, your body sometimes gives some good clues about which way to go. Even after you've done your homework, talked to many people and come up with a logical choice, it is possible that your impulse is telling you to go with the other choice. Don't be afraid to trust it. Very often your subconscious mind sends knowing messages as to which choice is better at a particular time. As you start paying attention to your impulses, you will be surprised at the good advice you are giving yourself.

I was surprised when I "trusted my gut" and found a new career. My intention after getting my doctorate in psychology was to ultimately set up a private practice. A few months after I began treating patients in a mental-health clinic the opportunity opened for me to help a friend who had become executive director of a marvelous health facility called "The Floating Hospital, New York's Ship of Health."* My instinct told me to take the job even though it didn't logically fit into the plans I had made for myself. Something within me said, "Go for it."

Within months, my friend resigned, and I was made executive director. Nowhere in my plan was it written that I would become an administrator. Previously, I had viewed myself as a follower, not a leader, and the whole concept of being at the helm had never entered my mind. Somehow my subconscious knew I could handle it and pushed me to take the job. "What am I doing here?" I asked myself as I went through fear and uncertainty in handling the tasks of the position. But as I learned and grew with the job, I realized I loved administrative work and, in fact, became very capable in that area. In addition, the Floating Hospital brought me rich, wonderful, crazy, hilarious, poignant and exciting experiences and challenges that I never thought would be possible for me. But my subconscious mind had known. It had overridden my conscious, logical mind, which had said, "Don't deviate from your plan" and "You can't handle this job."

I must make it clear, following the concept that there is no such thing as a wrong decision, that if I had chosen to remain a therapist in the mental-health clinic, *that choice also would have brought me rich opportunities for experiencing life in a new and different way.* There was no right or wrong decision, just different ones.

5. *Lighten up.* We live in a world where most people take themselves and their decisions very seriously. I have news for you. Nothing is *that* important. Honestly! If as a result

---

*At the time, The Floating Hospital was located aboard a ship and sailed around Manhattan while delivering healthcare services to the poor. After September 11, 2001, the ship was sold as it was unable to secure affordable and accessible dock space. It is now land-based and continues to deliver its services to the poor.

of a decision you make, you lose some money, no problem – you learn to deal with losing money. If you lose a lover, no problem – you find another one. If you choose to divorce, no problem – you learn to handle living on your own. If you choose to marry, no problem – you learn to handle a new kind of sharing.

Start thinking about yourself as a lifetime student at a large university. Your curriculum is your total relationship with the world you live in, from the moment you're born to the moment you die. Each experience is a valuable lesson to be learned. If you choose Path A, you will learn one set of lessons. If you choose Path B, you will learn a different set of lessons. Geology or geometry – just a different teacher and different books to read, different homework to do, different exams to take. *It really doesn't matter.* If you take Path A, you get to taste the strawberries. If you take Path B, you get to taste the blueberries. If you hate both strawberries and blueberries, you can find another path. The trick is simply to make whatever place you're in your educational forum and learn everything you can about yourself and the world around you. So – *lighten up!* Whatever happens as a result of your decision, *you'll handle it!*

After Making a Decision

1. *Throw away your picture.* We all create expectations of what we would like to happen after a decision is made. The picture in our mind's eye might have served a valuable function in helping to make a decision. But once the decision is made, let the picture go. Since you can't control the future, the picture can create unhappiness if it's not fulfilled. Disappointment may make you miss the good that can come out of every situation in which you find yourself. Don't forget to look for that silver lining. If you see the outcome of a decision as looking a certain way, you will increase the likelihood of missing other opportunities. Yet

the unexpected opportunities can create more of value than
your original picture. If you are focused on "the way it's
supposed to be," you might miss the opportunity to enjoy
the way it is or to have it be wonderful in a totally different
way from what you imagined.

2. *Accept total responsibility for your decisions.* This is a
tough one! We all have a tendency to look around for some
one to blame if things are not working out to our liking. I
really hated my stockbroker when the stock he
recommended went down instead of up. It took great
fortitude to admit to myself, "I made the decision to buy. No
one twisted my arm." I lamented until I created an
"opportunity" from my ill-fated decision. What did I learn?
A lot! I learned I had to find out more about the stock
market, instead of relying totally on my stockbroker's
opinion. I learned that I was terribly insecure about money,
and had to work on that. I learned I could lose money in the
stock market and yet life went on just as it did before. I
learned that if in the future I lost money in the stock market,
it wouldn't be such a big deal, and that stocks can go up
again, as mine did eight months later. When looked at in
that light, it wasn't a bad decision after all. When you can
find the *opportunity* in any decision, it is much easier
to accept the *responsibility* for making it.

When you take responsibility for your decisions, you
become a lot less angry at the world, and, most important, a
lot less angry at yourself!

3. *Don't protect, correct.* It is most important to commit
yourself to any decision you make and give it all you've got.
But if it doesn't work out, *change it!* Many of us are so
invested in making the "right" decision that even if we find
we don't like the path we have chosen, we hang in there for
dear life. To my way of thinking, this is the height of craziness. There is tremendous value in learning you *don't* like

something. Then it is simply a matter of changing your path. Yes, there are those who keep flitting from place to place, using "change it" as an excuse for noncommitment. I'm not talking about that, and you'll know the difference within yourself. If you've truly committed yourself to something, given it everything you've got, and then concluded that it is not for you – move on to something else.

When you decide to change paths, you will often face criticism from those around you. "What do you mean you want to change your career? You've invested five years in building up your dental practice! All that time and money down the drain!" Explain that none of it has been a waste. At one time it was the right thing for you to do. Much was learned and much was gained in the way of experience. It simply doesn't feel right any more – it's time to change. I know many people who stay locked in unsatisfactory situations that no longer work for them because they've invested so much and it would be a shame not to continue. How illogical! Why invest more, if it's no longer paying off? Remember – the quality of your life is at stake!

In his book *Actualizations,* Stewart Emery presents an excellent model for changing your direction in life. He learned it while seated on the flight deck of an airplane on the way to Honolulu. He noticed a console, which was identified by the pilot as the inertial guidance system. The purpose of the system was to get the plane within one thousand yards of the runway in Hawaii within five minutes of the estimated arrival time. Each time the plane strayed off course, the system corrected it. The pilot explained that they would arrive in Hawaii on time in spite of *"having been in error 90 percent of the time."* Emery takes it from there, stating: "So the path from here to where we want to be starts with an error, which we correct, which becomes the next error, which we correct and that becomes the next error, which we correct. So the only time we are truly on course is that moment in the zigzag when we actually cross the true path." From the analogy, we see that the trick in life is not to worry about making a wrong decision; *it's learning when to correct*! My concept of the model looks like this:

OFF COURSE/CORRECT MODEL

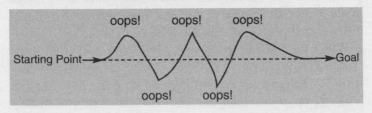

There are many inner clues that help you know when it is time to correct. The two most obvious are confusion and dissatisfaction. Ironically, these are considered negatives, instead of positives. I know it is hard to accept, but *an upset in your life is beneficial,* in that it tells you that you are off course in some way and you need to find your way back to your particular path of clarity once again. Your confusion and dissatisfaction are telling you that you're off-track, and, as the Chinese proverb says, "If you don't change your direction, you're likely to end up where you're heading."

Physical pain is easily seen as beneficial, even though it can be very uncomfortable. It is an obvious symptom that something is wrong with your body. A pain in your right side might save your life by signaling an appendicitis attack. If you don't pay attention to it, you could die. Mental pain is just as much a "blessing," because it is telling you that something is wrong with the way your life is going. It is a sign that something needs correction – whether it is the way you think about the world or what you are doing in the world – or both. The pain is simply saying, "Hey, that's not it!"

The way to figure out how to get back on course is through the exploration process – reaching out through self-help books, workshops, friends, support groups, therapy or whatever seems right for you when you reach out for help.

As long as you are open to reaching out, help will be there. Remember, "When the student is ready, the teacher will appear." You will never be ready if you are busy protecting the course you have chosen for yourself. You will be perpetually off course and never reach your destination. When you are constantly aware of the clues that signal "time to correct," you will always end up in the right spot – or at least in the vicinity.

As a handy review, here is a summary of the steps in the decision-making process. By applying these, you'll breathe a lot easier as you make choices throughout your lifetime.

NO-LOSE DECISION-MAKING PROCESS

BEFORE MAKING A DECISION
1. Focus on the No-Lose Model.
2. Do your homework.
3. Establish your priorities.
4. Trust your impulses.
5. Lighten up.

AFTER MAKING A DECISION
1. Throw away your picture.
2. Accept total responsibility.
3. Don't protect, correct.

If you don't think the above makes absolute sense, let me summarize the steps we usually take when using the No-Win Model:

NO-WIN DECISION-MAKING PROCESS

BEFORE MAKING A DECISION
1. Focus on the No-Win Model.
2. Listen to your mind drive you crazy.
3. Paralyze yourself with anxiety as you try to predict the future.

4. Don't trust your impulses – listen to what everyone else thinks.
5. Feel the heaviness of having to make a decision.

AFTER MAKING A DECISION
1. Create anxiety by trying to control the outcome.
2. Blame someone else if it doesn't work out as you pictured.
3. If it does work out, keep wondering if it would have been better the other way.
4. Don't correct if the decision is "wrong" – you have too much invested.

Does this last summary sound painfully (and comically) familiar? Yes, we certainly do know how to drive ourselves crazy!

Now that I've demonstrated the No-Win and No-Lose Models as they pertain to decision making, I trust you can see how it is impossible to make a mistake. Just as each decision is an opportunity to learn, each "mistake" is also an opportunity to learn, rendering it impossible to make a mistake. A great researcher, having "failed" two hundred times before he found the answer to one of his burning questions, was asked, "Doesn't it bother you that you failed all those times?" His answer was, "I never failed! I discovered two hundred ways *not* to do something!"

After much consideration, I have come to the conclusion that if you haven't made any mistakes lately, you must be doing something wrong. You'll never get to Hawaii! You haven't even left the airport yet! You've never even gotten off the ground! You are taking no risks – nor are you enjoying the "goodies" life has to offer. What a waste!

I remember a time in my life when I was frightened of just about everything – fearful that I would fail in all my attempts to fulfill my dreams. So I just stayed home, a victim of all my insecurities. I'd like to report that it was an ancient Zen master who snapped me back into awareness. But it wasn't. It was actually an airline commercial that used the slogan "Get into this world." When I saw the commercial, I suddenly realized that I had stopped participating in the world. With this "enlightenment," I started pushing myself out there once again. I realized I had to shift from being afraid of making a mistake to being afraid of *not* making a mistake. If I am not making any mistakes, I can be sure I am not learning and growing.

When you consider that mistakes are an integral part of living, it is amazing how we are taught to think we must be perfect. This "mistake" in our thinking has created many fears about being adventurous and trying out new territories. Let's take an example from a favorite national pastime, baseball. It is extremely rare for a baseball player to attain a .400 average. Translated, that means having a hit four times out of ten at bat – four successes out of ten tries. That's a champion's performance – and most of us are just beginners!

You are not going to succeed in everything you attempt in life. That's guaranteed. In fact, the more you do in life, the more chance there is *not* to succeed in some things. Look at how rich your life can be, however, from your many adventures. Win or lose, you just keep winning! Using the Off Course/Correct Model, you can now have a new freedom in flying.

Although you now know how to minimize your fears about decision making and making a mistake, you might notice that adopting the concepts presented are more difficult than they sound. Again I remind you of the lengthy process involved in behavior change. *Simply begin!* Keep working on it. Keep reinforcing the new way of thinking presented here by using the exercises below to help you push through your fears about making decisions or mistakes.

Are you making any mistakes lately? I hope so!

Exercises

1. Using the No-Lose Model, consider some decisions you are now facing. Write down all the positive things that can happen by using either pathway – even if the outcome might not be what you picture.

2. Learn the concept IT DOESN'T REALLY MATTER by starting with little decisions you face each day. As you ponder which suit to wear to the office, notice that it doesn't really matter; which restaurant to eat at tonight, it doesn't really matter; which movie to see, it doesn't really matter. Each choice simply produces a different experience. Slowly you will be able to apply this concept to larger and larger decisions. Put signs in your home and office that say

IT REALLY DOESN'T MATTER

to remind yourself when you are being needlessly obsessive.

3. Also, put signs in your home and office that say

SO WHAT! I'LL HANDLE IT!

If things don't work out the way you want, so what! What's the big deal, anyway? This reminder will help you lighten up about life as you learn you can handle whatever happens after you've made your decision.

4. Look at clues in your life that suggest you are off course and begin making your game plan to correct the situation.

8

How Whole Is Your "Whole Life"?

"I am devastated without Jim. He was my whole life!" Louise was one of my students whose husband had just divorced her after five years of marriage. She wasn't kidding when she said that Jim was her whole life, for that's exactly what she had made him. Nothing or no one else had any real significance.

This, of course, explains her devastation and desperate sense of emptiness when he left. It probably also explains, in part, the breakdown of the marriage. As I explain in *The Feel the Fear Guide to Lasting Love*, dependency in a relationship creates some very unattractive side effects – anger, jealousy, resentment, clinging, nagging – all very unpleasant to live with. These self-defeating qualities are the result of a deep-seated fear of losing that which we see as the basis of our entire identity.

Bob, a public-relations executive, chose to create his identity in the area of *work*. For him, there was only his career; nothing else mattered. As with Louise, negative side effects accompanied his emotional dependency. At work, he was protective instead of expansive and giving; he usurped credit for everything, ignoring the contributions of those with whom he worked; and in his constant attempt to gain approval from his superiors, he never took a chance. Thus his creativity was greatly diminished.

When he lost his job because of a series of cutbacks, he predictably experienced a feeling of devastation, an extreme sense of helplessness, and thoughts of suicide – all brought on by a horrible feeling of emptiness. His lifeline had been severed.

Men and an increasing number of women who have lived their entire adult years emotionally tied to their work often fall apart when they are forced to retire. It is as though their lives are over – in fact, many die soon after their retirement begins. How sad that they cannot enjoy what is potentially the most enjoyable and creative part of their lives!

Jeanne, a housewife, made her *children* the totality of her life. To those who didn't understand, she looked like, and believed herself to be, a "good" mother. She was always there when the children came home from school, she catered to their every need, and she prided herself on the fact that her children always came first.

If Jeanne had been more honest with herself, she would have seen she was using her children to create her reason to exist. Those who really knew her were aware of the inevitable side effects – a need to dominate, overprotectiveness, self-righteousness, and the creation of massive amounts of guilt in her children. She never let them forget what a giving person she was. When they grew up and eventually went off on their own, Jeanne faced what she perceived as a totally empty house – despite the fact that she and her husband still lived there. This mirrored the total emptiness she felt inside. Staying home with children is not inherently bad. However, when parents depend on children for their own emotional survival, it is clearly detrimental. Not only is it unhealthy for the parent; it is also unhealthy for the children. A parent's survival is a heavy burden for a child to bear!

The underlying feeling that Louise, Bob and Jeanne shared was an extreme sense of neediness. When they lost the things in their lives to which they were emotionally tied, this neediness was exposed. I will wager that most of you, at some time or another, have experienced this same kind of neediness. If so, you will agree it is one of the most painful feelings you can experience. And to make matters worse, when you are in the throes of desperation, there seems to be little you can do to make yourself feel better.

This raises a question: Is there anything that can be done to help loosen the grip of this intense neediness, that can make us feel whole despite a great loss in our life? If there is, imagine how greatly our fear of loss could be diminished. The answer to this question is undeniably YES! That should come as a relief.

Although you should be ecstatic that relief is possible, it is important to keep in mind that, as with everything else associated with change, it takes a great deal of awareness, patience and perseverance to break strong emotion-backed patterns. This should not worry you. While it may sound like an unpleasant task, it really isn't, *if* you take it in small and manageable steps and allow yourself time really to enjoy the process.

So I invite you to try an alternate way of handling your life; it is geared toward helping you release the desperation, emptiness and fear that may be attached to certain aspects of your life. I know from my own experience that this release is possible. This chapter spells out the steps necessary for change. I promise you these steps offer some interesting insights. Yet only through action and commitment can they become powerful tools that will absolutely change the quality of your life.

It will be helpful first for you to understand more clearly what I consider to be the cause of the emptiness you feel when your life is out of balance. Using RELATIONSHIP as an example, the following illustrates what your Whole Life looks like when you focus emotionally on only one area:

WHOLE LIFE WITH RELATIONSHIP

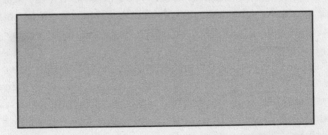

RELATIONSHIP

If, as in Louise's case, the big R disappears, life suddenly looks like this:

WHOLE LIFE WITHOUT RELATIONSHIP

No wonder you feel empty! No wonder you have the urge to replace that relationship immediately! There's nothing left!

It doesn't have to be this way. Look at the following Whole Life, which represents an entirely different way of seeing things:

WHOLE LIFE WITH RELATIONSHIP

Contribution	Hobby	Leisure
Family	Alone Time	Personal Growth
Work	Relationship	Friends

This represents the Whole Life of another one of my students, Nancy. Taking the form of a grid, instead of a vacuous box, life looks amazingly different for Nancy than for poor Louise, Bob and Jeanne. Not only is Nancy's grid filled with nourishment and aliveness, but the entire area of her Life seems to have increased, which, in effect, gives her more for her money. Let's assume that Nancy, too, experiences the loss of her love. What does her Whole Life look like then? What a difference compared with Louise's loss! You will notice from the following grid that the loss of Nancy's relationship leaves a hole. But it hardly wipes her out! Yes, there was pain when Nancy split from her boyfriend; yes, she is lonely at times; and yes, she would like eventually to have a successful relationship. Yet,

WHOLE LIFE WITHOUT RELATIONSHIP

Contribution	Hobby	Leisure
Family	Alone Time	Personal Growth
Work		Friends

without it, her life still works beautifully. Each day is filled with a multitude of experiences that bring her joy and satisfaction; hence, her neediness is gone. There are so many resources available to her that she truly feels as if life is a giant cornucopia that will never be empty.

At this point in one of my classes a student piped up to say that she, too, has many things in her life – family, children, job, friends – but the only thing that *means* anything to her is relationship. I pointed out that this is where the awareness, perseverance and patience come in – to enhance the *commitment* she has to each area of her life.

Commitment, as I am using the term, means consciously giving 100% – everything you've got – to each "box" of the grid. For example, when you are at work, work full out, holding nothing back; when you are with your family, consciously be *with* them, 100%; when you are with friends, be there 100% . . . and so on.

As I started explaining commitment to my class, Sandy, another student, immediately responded that her job was only temporary, until she found something better. In the meantime, she was bored out of her mind and couldn't wait to leave it. Therefore, how could she possibly commit herself to being there 100%? I explained that commitment doesn't mean it has to last forever, but *while you are there* commit yourself 100%. By doing this, the quality of your life will improve 100%.

I gave her a tool to use on the job to enhance the concept of commitment. This tool is to *"act as if" you really count.* What would that look like? What would she be doing if she knew she really counted? Some possibilities the class came up with were: creating daily goals and seeing that they are completed, interacting with other staff members in a way that would make their day happier, creating an environment that is a pleasure to work in. She added, "I would also get there on time." Sandy promised she would give it a try after I assured her that committing herself to this job would not mean that she would be there forever.

Sandy returned to class the following week very excited about what had transpired. We were all struck by the increased level of her energy. She reported that she had taken a plant and a painting to work, which immediately brightened her little area. She was complimentary and helpful to the people around her, and each night before she left the office she created goals to complete the following day. As each day progressed, she focused on her goals and was amazed to find she now got twice as much done each day. She got addicted to the act of checking off her goals

– it felt so good. When on the rare occasion she didn't get to something on the list, she merely carried it over to the next day.

Sandy was amazed at the response. One of her co-workers actually asked her what she was on, and said, "Whatever it is, continue taking it!" But the magical result was that *she actually began to enjoy her job.* Participating 100% eliminates boredom. Once Sandy got over her "woe is me" attitude and began to choose to be there 100%, a feeling of satisfaction and aliveness resulted. Her "acting as if" she counts is creating other benefits as well: increased self-esteem, a good reference when she finally does move on to another job and the realization that she actually can make a difference. This, of course, makes her feel more powerful in a world where so many people feel helpless.

To make commitment a less heavy concept, keep in mind that, contrary to what we have been taught, it doesn't necessarily mean forever.

For example, my job as the executive director of The Floating Hospital brought me a great deal of joy and satisfaction, but after eight years I began to feel I was ready for another kind of challenge. Since I was totally committed to The Floating Hospital, I was determined that it would operate just as smoothly after my departure as before. I began breaking in someone to replace me. I began delegating more and more. I gradually familiarized the board of trustees with the new person I thought would be perfect for the job. I prepared everyone for my leaving. So you see that, even though I was on my way out, I was committed to that job 100%.

At the same time, I was totally committed to having my life work after I left my job. In my free hours, I began teaching, writing and increasing my private psychotherapy practice. In two years, the groundwork had been laid for the future of both The Floating Hospital and my new career. I was ready to leave.

The same principle works in the area of relationship. No one really knows how long any given relationship will last. But until you decide to let it go, it is important that you give your mate and yourself the respect and dignity you both deserve by committing yourself to be there 100%. If the day arises when you know that it is time to split, you will know that you gave it everything you had. And if, for some reason, your mate decides to end the relationship, you will know you did your best. There is nothing to regret. If you have already incorporated the grid concept into your life, the loss will not be enormous, since you have so many other areas of nourishment in your life.

One area of the grid needs some explanation: the area of CONTRIBUTION. This is the area that allows you to make your own special difference in the world. Contribution is discussed in a later chapter; for now, simply note that it is from the area of contribution that much of your self-esteem and satisfaction in life can come. To know that you can make a difference in this world means that you are not helpless, that you are a meaningful force in the world.

It is important that you don't think of contribution in such grand terms as those of Gandhi, Martin Luther King, Jr., or Albert Einstein. Contribution in the way that I am using it means beginning exactly where you are, looking around, seeing what needs to be done, and doing it. This could relate to your family, your friends, your community, your country, the world. There is not a person alive who is not capable of greatly contributing to the well-being of this planet. Just changing your attitude can affect the world around you.

Now that you understand the concept of the grid and recognize its importance in reducing many of your fears regarding relationship, job, children, and so on, you are ready to take steps to incorporate this powerful tool into your daily life. Here are the steps:

1. Simply recognize that you might be caught in a vicious circle. If you look carefully at your past, you will probably notice that every time negative feelings associated with loss came up, you took the very same pathway to try to relieve the discomfort: You tried to re-create that which you had lost.

For example, what's the first thing many of us do when we are devastated by the loss of a loved one? We simply substitute heads. And when the next love of our life leaves, we experience the same feeling of devastation (which is amazing, since we've only known this lover for three weeks). Then what do we do? It's not hard to guess – we go out and find another "one and only" without whom we would simply die!

If this or a similar pattern sounds familiar, it is important not to make a big thing out of it. Just recognize that up until now you simply did not have an appropriate framework within which to create a healthier way to act. The mere fact that you acknowledge the possibility of another way is enough to get you to the next step.

2. Create your own Whole Life Grid. Begin by making a nine-boxed square like the one on page 130.

Take some time to think about what components you would like to include in your life and begin filling in the boxes. I am a great believer in setting the stage whenever I begin any kind of introspection, so I recommend that you play some calming music in the background while you are filling in the boxes. Make sure you are alone and that the phone is turned off.

3. After you have filled in your grid, pick one of the boxes to work on. Shut your eyes and visualize what you would like that part of your life to look like. What would you be doing? How would you be interacting with the people around you? How would it feel? Remember the two key ingredients: 100% commitment and acting as if you count. Let's call them the MAGIC DUO, for that's exactly what they create in your life – magic.

PERSONAL WHOLE LIFE

4. When you get a clear picture, take a blank piece of paper and begin writing down what your mind created for you, paying attention to all the details. This will help you with Step 5.

5. List the many things that would have to be done in order to make your visualization become a reality. Again, take time to think this through carefully. I cannot repeat too frequently:

ACTION IS THE KEY TO YOUR SUCCESS.

You have to *do* something to make your real life match your visualization. So your actions are critical.

Let's see how this might actually work. If you had picked the area PERSONAL GROWTH, you might see yourself taking classes and workshops, reading books and attending lectures. In your visualization, the Magic Duo assures that you will approach all of this with a will that keeps you focused, and also assures your active participation at all times.

If you are in a workshop, you might see yourself interacting with the other students, doing all the homework, whether it is a credit course or not, happily anticipating the next class and really happy that you have chosen to be there.

By the way, when you take this concept into the real world, old habits will emerge – that's a given! Thus, when you are actually at a workshop, you might suddenly be overcome by the wish that you were with *him*. In the beginning, your mind will *definitely, without a question*, want to pull you out of your commitment, and it will take your constant vigilance to control the wandering. Eventually you will be able to say, "The heck with him – I'm here to learn!" Imagine what this does for your self-esteem! Eventually you will be able to make your mind focus on the matter at hand and take in what is happening around you. And then guess what happens! The neediness begins to disappear. The problem with needy people is that they can't take in anything around them. Then they wonder why they are starving emotionally.

What about the area of FRIENDS? What would that look like? Here, you might see yourself inviting them over for dinner, creating a terrific evening out, writing them letters of appreciation, or simply calling them and telling them you were thinking about them. In the real world, when with your friends you will probably wish you were with your one-and-only. This is the time to call in the Magic Duo. Begin by focusing on your commitment to be a wonderful friend, "acting as if" you truly make a difference in their lives.

From that mental place, you will begin to find much pleasure and fulfillment.

When I was a young woman, my friends and I had an unwritten contract: "I'll keep my date with you as long as Mr. Wonderful doesn't call." Although everyone seemed to have understood the rule, looking back I consider it a lousy policy – stupid, as well, since I always had such a great time with my girlfriends. As I matured I stopped treating my friends with such disrespect. An interesting side effect was that I ceased being considered a last-minute date by the male population. The men in my life began phoning days and sometimes weeks in advance when they knew I would not cancel other commitments to be with them.

Let's look at the area of LEISURE. This one stumps a lot of my students, and I admit it is an area I must work on daily. Many of us tend to be achievement-oriented and get anxious when taking time to relax and enjoy ourselves. It seems to be okay when you're relaxing with your mate or friends, but when on your own, you feel you should be accomplishing something. Again, the way to release this anxiety is to call upon the Magic Duo. By committing yourself 100% to your relaxation and "acting as if" your well-being counts, you can enjoy taking some time alone for yourself.

To help myself out, I've created the concept of the holi-hour, a shortened version of the holi-day. I allow myself at least an hour each day to relax totally. It could mean reading magazines, walking on the beach, or shopping in my favorite mall. This helps greatly in keeping me refreshed in my work. Very often I get some of my best ideas during leisure time, when my mind is not so cluttered.

6. Do steps 3, 4 and 5 for every area of your grid. You will be amazed at what a beautiful life begins to emerge – so rich, full, loving and giving. It is important to keep in mind

that whatever you create in your grid can become a reality
– if you are commited to taking the necessary action.

7. Each day, create for yourself specific goals that reflect all
the boxes in your grid. If you are already a diligent daily
goal setter, you will probably notice that your goals are
focused in only one area of your life – most likely work. By
setting goals for all areas of your grid, your life will become
balanced.

As you approach each goal, bear in mind the Magic Duo
– *100% commitment* and *I count* – to help you focus and
achieve a sense of fulfillment.

You may not be able to cover every area of your grid
every day. Naturally, there will be times in your life when
one area takes precedence. For example, when on vacation
you can forget about other areas of the grid. Just concentrate
on having a good time. The Magic Duo will ensure that you
take it all in. In the same manner, an important work project
may require your undivided attention for a time. What you
are ultimately looking for is overall balance.

Consider this: If you don't feel like taking the time or
making the effort to do these steps, you will be greatly
shortchanging yourself. Isn't your life worth it? What I'm
asking you to do is to set up the basic structure of your life,
so you can then go on living in a way that supports your
growth and satisfaction. As Janet, one of my students, so
aptly put it, "If you always do what you've always done,
you'll always get what you've always got." This thought
certainly served to get her moving!

If you find it difficult to motivate yourself, don't put
yourself down. Find a self-help group to act as a catalyst. If
you can't find a support group, find what I call a "growth
buddy." You and your buddy can help each other by
meeting weekly and working on the grid, your goals, your
action plan, or whatever. Committing yourself to do certain
homework before each meeting often spurs you on to

action. The key is to take your commitment to your buddy seriously and act responsibly during the week by getting everything done that you committed yourself to do.

If you can't find a self-help group and do not want to work with a growth buddy, find a group conducted by a professional. It is amazing how quickly results materialize when you know what you want and are determined to get it. Most people never take the time to focus on what they want – then they wonder why they always feel empty.

Keep asking yourself, "How whole is my life?" Continue to create such richness for yourself that nothing can ever take away your basic sense of completeness. Can you imagine how little you would then have to fear?

9

**Just Nod Your Head
– Say "Yes!"**

One of the most valuable lessons in learning to diminish fear is embodied in the phrase SAY YES TO YOUR UNIVERSE. These words were casually uttered by Janet Zuckerman, a wonderful teacher of mine, to someone who was complaining bitterly about a particular circumstance in his life. I asked Janet exactly what she meant by that phrase, and she replied, "It's simple. Whatever happens to you in life, just nod your head, up and down, instead of shaking it, side to side. Just say *yes* instead of no." Over the years I've incorporated this phrase into my life with magical results.

The term "universe" refers to that life plan that seems to take over despite what we have in mind – that "force" operating, seemingly on its own, that often interferes with our picture of how we would like things to be. It refers to a certain flow in our lives and the lives of others over which we have little or no control. So often when we are all set to move in a specific direction, an unexpected event changes everything. Those unexpected events or even the *possibility* of the unexpected sets us up for a great deal of fear. We anticipate the worst. It is important to remember:

In saying "yes" lies the antidote to our fear.

The phrase "say yes" means "to agree to" those things that life hands us. Saying *yes* means letting go of resistance and letting in the possibilities that our universe offers in new ways of seeing the world. It means to relax bodily, and calmly survey the situation, thereby reducing upset and anxiety. Aside from the emotional benefits, the physical benefits are enormous. Conversely, saying *no* means to be a victim. "How could this happen to me!" Saying no means to block, to fight, to resist opportunities for growth and challenge. Saying *no* creates tension, exhaustion, wasted expenditure of energy, emotional upheaval – or, worse, it creates apathy. "I can't cope. I can't go on. There is no hope." The truth of the matter is that saying *yes* is our only hope.

Not only is saying *yes* our antidote to dealing with day-to-day disappointments, rejections, and missed opportunities (the flu, a leaking roof, a traffic jam, a flat tire, a lousy date, and so on), *it is the miracle tool for dealing with our deepest, darkest fears*.

Let me tell you about Charles, whose presence in my life confirmed the power of saying *yes* to the universe. Charles grew up in poverty in a New York ghetto. His "tough guy" image served him well until he was severely handicapped by a gunshot wound incurred in a street fight. His spine was shattered, and he was paralyzed from the waist down.

When I met Charles, he had just completed training in a rehabilitation center and was looking for a job at The Floating Hospital. Charles wanted an opportunity to teach children how to avoid getting into trouble the way he had. He became part of my staff and an inspiration to everyone around him.

One day I walked into one of our classrooms and found Charles sitting with a group of children surrounding him. He was answering all the burning questions that young people have when they look at a handicapped person. "What does it feel like not to be able to walk?" "What should I say to someone in a wheelchair?" "How do you go to the bathroom?" At one point, Charles asked the group what they thought a handicapped person wanted most. One little boy quickly answered, "Friends!" "Right!" answered Charles, and all the children spontaneously jumped up and hugged him, shouting, "I'll be your friend!" I don't know who got more out of the session – Charles, the children, or me.

On another occasion, we were giving a party for a new group of senior citizens. Although we had hired a three-piece band for the festivities, the seniors were hesitant about getting into the swing of things. All of a sudden, Charles pushed his chair into the middle of the room and started "dancing" with the music. "Come on, everyone. If I can get out here and dance, so can you." Within minutes, he had everyone dancing, laughing, singing and clapping. His spirit was infectious. The strangers in the room quickly became friends. He never missed the opportunity to show people that, with a positive attitude, value can be created from anything that happens to you in life.

I had many opportunities to talk with Charles. He told me that in the early days of his disability he had lost all hope, all will. As he described it, "It wasn't easy for a macho kid to lose his ability to walk, let alone to lose all control of his bladder and bowels." He was referred to an excellent rehabilitation center, but refused to be helped. The center was about to send him home to make way for someone who was willing to take responsibility for his own life. That was the turning point. Charles knew that if he was sent home, he would have no chance at all. This was his moment to say *yes* or *no* to his universe. He is thankful he chose to say *yes*.

Once that choice was made, his progress was remarkable. Opportunities opened up to him that he'd never thought about before. He decided that his life could have a purpose: to help others in their struggle, whatever that struggle might be. He would be a model, saying, "If I could do it, so can you." Charles admitted to me that, strangely, he was grateful now for his handicap, because it made him aware of how much he had to contribute to the world.

Before the accident, Charles had been blind to the fact that his life had meaning. Now he believes he was more handicapped before the accident; only since then has he derived satisfaction from living.

When I presented the concept of SAY YES TO YOUR UNIVERSE in class, one of my students asked an interesting question: "If you always say *yes* to your universe, wouldn't you be able to avoid feeling any pain?" I thought about it for a moment and told him no. You can't avoid pain, but you can say *yes* to the pain, understanding that it is a part of life. You do not, then, feel yourself a victim. You know that you can handle the pain, as well as the situation causing the pain. You do not feel it is hopeless. At that point, my student shouted, "I get it! You mean there is the pain of *yes* versus the pain of *no*." That was exactly what I meant.

As the class looked at it further, they were able to find examples of when they had said *yes* to pain in their lives without realizing what they were doing. Nadine remembered one day the previous week when she thought about her mother, who had recently died. Suddenly she was struck by the pain of loss. She sat down and cried, thinking how strangely sweet it felt to remember back to good times she had shared with her mother. And as she cried, she felt the urge to say "thanks" over and over again.

She was aware, in the middle of her pain, that life hands you a lot of good-byes – but that's just the way life is. Yet she saw the difference between handling the death of a loved one as a catastrophe (saying *no*) and keeping in mind how blessed she was to have had that person in her life (saying *yes*). It is seeing death as part of living – a natural process – as opposed to seeing it as a horrible deprivation and unjust phenomenon.

Betsy, another student, remembered the sweetness of the pain she felt as she kissed her son good-bye when he went off to college. With tears in her eyes, she watched him walk down the path to his new car, knowing he would return again only as a visitor. It was now time to let him go. She reported thinking, *yes,* this is the way life is . . . always changing. Things don't last forever. She let herself cry for a while, but soon picked herself up and decided to prepare a candlelit dinner. After all, she and her husband would be alone for the first time in many years, so she was determined to make a honeymoon of it.

Compare this with a parent who dreads her children leaving home, and when it finally happens is able to see only the emptiness of the house and the uselessness of her life. Such a person, resisting change, misses the new pathways opening up for her. Betsy's story beautifully demonstrates the ability to feel pain when something ends but then to go on and build new hopes and dreams for oneself. There is something enriching about leaving one beautiful experience in your life and looking forward to other beautiful experiences.

Marge shared with the class the pain she felt when her husband died. Yes, she missed her husband and the warmth and companionship he had given her, but she was also aware of how she had transformed herself from a dependent to an independent person when left to her own resources. Her sense of self-esteem had increased enormously as she slowly learned to take risks she had never taken before. She was able to say *yes* to life and create a whole new world for herself.

Marge could have reacted like a friend of mine did. He refused to pick up the pieces and go on after his wife died. Five years later, he is still crying on the phone, asking, "Why did she have to die?" He has said *no* to his universe. Unfortunately, he doesn't see that the universe isn't suffering, only he is, and perhaps the few people who still talk to him on the phone. He has refused to see the blessings in his life – and there are many – or the opportunities around him to meet new people and try new experiences. The pain of *no* leaves him feeling powerless.

In the final analysis, it can be said that your ability to cope effectively with the world around you corresponds to your ability to say *yes* to your universe, including the pain. Remember:

**Acknowledgment of pain is very important;
denial is deadly.**

Sandy is someone who avoided her pain. When her son died in an automobile accident twelve years ago, she never faced the full impact of the loss. Friends remarked on how well she had handled her son's death. Three years later, she developed epilepsy, which seemed to be unrelated to the loss she had experienced. For nine years she suffered from seizures that prevented her from working. In addition, her relationships with her husband and other children were slowly deteriorating.

Sandy finally went to a support group to get help in dealing with the upset the epilepsy was creating within the family. During the first session, the group leader asked if she had ever suffered a great loss. She said yes, but explained that it had happened so long ago it was no longer a factor in her life. He knew better and with great skill managed to get her back into the experience of her son's death. It was then that she finally allowed her grief to emerge.

Each time the group met, Sandy continued to deal with her pain. Almost "miraculously," her epileptic symptoms disappeared within five weeks. She discontinued her medication, found a good job and began to repair the damage done within her home as a result of her illness. Pain can be incredibly destructive if kept submerged. Although Sandy's is a dramatic example, unacknowledged pain is subtly destroying many people's lives.

We all know people who are out of touch with their pain – who have refused to let themselves feel their emotions. When we don't acknowledge our pain, it will be transferred into a bodily symptom, anger or something equally destructive. Saying *yes* means letting in the pain full force, knowing you will not only get to the other side of it, but also gain something in the end – if you look for it.

As the class discussions continued, my students and I came up with an interesting thought: the richer our lives, the more likely we are to experience the pain of loss. If we have a multitude of friends, we will have to deal with more goodbyes. The more we are able to reach out into the world, the greater the likelihood is that we are going to experience "failure" or rejection. But those who are living rich lives wouldn't change them for a moment. They delight in the opportunity to taste all that life has to offer – the good and the bad. The class also decided that it is likely that those who lead rich lives intuitively know the secret of saying *yes* to the universe. Those who say no usually withdraw from life, choosing symbolically to hide under the covers to keep themselves from becoming victims – ironically, ending up complete victims of their own fears.

I found the most extreme and moving example of saying *yes* in the pages of Viktor Frankl's book *Man's Search for Meaning*. It was given to me by a friend, who said "I think it's really important for you to read this book."

I was upset to learn that the book was about Frankl's experience in a concentration camp – a subject I had carefully avoided. It was simply too frightening for me to look at. I had viewed life in a concentration camp as the most terrible experience a human being could endure – mentally, physically and spiritually. I really didn't want to read this book, and was about to put it aside when my friend's words came back to me: "I think it's really important for you to read this book." She obviously knew something I didn't, so I decided to find out what she was talking about.

I painfully pushed through page after page of descriptions that defied human comprehension. I couldn't keep back my tears. But as I continued to read, my heart slowly started to lighten. Not only had Frankl and others like him faced life in a concentration camp, but, according to the definition given earlier, *they had actually said yes to their universe!* They were able to create a positive experience out of what life had handed them. They were able to find personal meaning and growth – and a way of seeing the world that created value from their experience. As Frankl wrote:

> The experiences of camp life show that a man does have a choice of action. There were enough examples, often of a heroic nature, which proved that apathy could be overcome, irritability suppressed. Man *can* preserve a vestige of spiritual freedom, of independence of mind, even in such terrible conditions of psychic and physical stress. We who lived in concentration camps can remember the men who walked through the huts comforting others, giving away their last piece of bread. They may have been few in number, but they offer sufficient proof that everything can be taken away from a man but one thing: the last of the human freedoms – to choose one's attitude in any given set of circumstances, to choose one's way. The way in which a man accepts his fate and all the suffering it entails, the way in which he takes up his cross, gives him ample opportunity – even in the most difficult circumstances – to add a deeper meaning to his life.

As I finished the last page, I knew that a dramatic change had taken place within me. I would never again experience fear with the same intensity I had experienced it before reading the book. I knew that if Frankl was able to create something positive out of his experience, which was the worst my mind could imagine, then I – and everyone else – could create value out of anything life could possibly hand me. It is a matter of remaining conscious that we have the choice.

I am sure that, given the option, Frankl would have preferred not to go through the experience, but the concentration camp was what life handed him. It was then up to him to create his reaction to the situation. We can't control the world, but we can control our reactions to it. I think you now begin to see how SAY YES TO YOUR UNIVERSE can work, not only to reduce fear, but also to create meaning in life.

During another class, one of my students argued that if we say *yes* to everything, we are accepting everything. If we accept everything, then we won't act to change things that are wrong with this world. I explained to him that saying *yes* means positive action; saying *no* means giving up. It is only when we see *possibility* for change that we can work to effect change. We can say *no* to the situation as it is, but *yes* to the possibility for the growth it offers. If you believe a situation in your life is hopeless, you simply sit back and let yourself be destroyed.

On a global level, if you believe it is hopeless to halt nuclear annihilation, you won't get involved in standing up for peaceful solutions to the world's problems. If you know this situation is *not* hopeless, you say *yes* to the opportunity to get involved in the process of making ours a peaceful planet, as so many people are doing throughout the world. These people are not paralyzed by fear, because they are saying *yes* to the opportunities inherent in the situation.

Saying *yes* does not mean giving up.

Saying yes means getting up and acting on your belief that you can create meaning and purpose in whatever life hands you.

It means channeling resources to find constructive, healthy ways to deal with adverse situations. It means acting out of strength, not weakness. It means having the flexibility necessary to survey many options and choose ones that enhance growth. It does not mean being destroyed; it means becoming alive to possibility.

Whereas the concept of saying *yes* to your universe is fairly easy to grasp, learning to say *yes* requires a great deal of awareness. We seem to have an automatic reflex that pushes the *no* button. It is not so easy to understand how to say *yes* when a child is gravely ill, when you become physically disabled, when you lose your job or when your spouse dies. Remember:

> **The world is filled with people who have been
> handed the "worst" life has to offer . . .
> and they have come out winners!**

We are all winners when we say *yes,* and it is worth every effort to learn how. The following steps will help:

1. Create *awareness* that you are saying *no.* It helps to surround yourself with reminders. Put signs on your desk, on your night table, on your mirrors, in your daily calendar, or wherever you'll see them. Some signs that helped me were: SAY YES TO YOUR UNIVERSE (an obvious one); I AM FINDING VALUE IN EVERYTHING THAT HAPPENS TO ME; LET GO. My daughter gave me a wonderful poster that said, IF LIFE GIVES YOU LEMONS, MAKE LEMONADE. You can create your own sayings that work best for you. The object is to stay *conscious.* We are asleep on this issue and need constantly to be reminded.

2. Once consciousness is there, *actually nod your head up and down, say yes.* There is something about physically affirming an idea that helps to create acceptance. Try nodding your head right now. You'll notice you feel something positive about the feeling of physically nodding in agreement. It gives you the sense that everything will be all right – because you are going to make it all right.

3. Using the same principle, physically relax your body, starting from the top of your head and going to the tip of your toes. Notice where you are tense and focus on letting the tension go. Again the body can take the lead in setting up positive feelings. This is discussed later.

4. Look for ways to create value from any experience. Ask yourself these questions: What can I learn from the experience? How can I use this experience to positive advantage? How can I learn to better myself as a result of this experience? Simply having the intent to create something positive automatically ensures that something positive will happen. As discussed in Chapter 7, let go of the picture of what the outcome "should" be, to open the way for possibilities your mind is incapable of envisioning.

5. Be patient with yourself, DON'T SAY NO TO YOUR DIFFICULTY IN SAYING YES. This is one of those concepts that seems easy but requires diligence to put into practice. It is easy to feel frustrated when gloom and doom overtake you. Just keep noticing this. Trust that you'll eventually get bored being depressed or upset and you'll then find a way out of the quicksand. Most of us do anyway. Saying *yes* helps you find your way much faster, thus vastly improving the quality of your life.

One additional tip may be helpful. Start practicing on trivial events in your life. Although they may have nothing to do with fear, they will give you practice with the process. For example, as you sit in your car fuming because of a traffic jam, a sign on the dashboard that reads SAY YES TO YOUR UNIVERSE may remind you that you are saying *no*. Once you can create this awareness, you can nod your head, relax your body and begin to use the experience to some advantage. You can use such time to listen to some of the great "inspirational" audios that are available or an audio book you have no time to read. Or you can be grateful that for the moment nothing very taxing is demanded of you. So sit back and enjoy the experience.

If you are worried that you are keeping someone waiting, remember that there is nothing you can do about it, so you might as well relax. It is a perfect opportunity to learn that in the future you will need to allow more time for unexpected delays.

If you are on the other end, waiting, muttering to yourself, "He's late again!" focus on saying *yes* to the fact that you now have an opportunity to people-watch or reflect on the day's activities. I'm one of those people who loves to wait. It gives me a rare opportunity to do nothing without feeling guilty!

Life offers many opportunities to practice saying *yes* to your universe. The baby spills milk all over the floor; your secretary loses the letter you dictated; the cleaner ruins your suit – get the picture? Every time you find yourself resisting what's happening at the present moment, recall the phrase SAY YES TO YOUR UNIVERSE. You will watch your life become more and more pleasurable. Relationships with the whole world will improve dramatically.

Once you master the concept on a day-to-day level, you will be prepared to handle the more serious issues that confront you. You will notice your level of fear slowly starts to drop as it is replaced by a greater sense of trust in your ability to handle your world. As you start to see the possibilities in the impossible, you will begin to see that the world works "perfectly." You can find reason and purpose in everything – if you open your mind to it.

The only time you will fear anything is when you say *no* and resist the universe. You may have heard the expression "Get into the flow." This means consciously accepting what is happening in your life. I once heard it said that the key to life is not to figure out what you can *get from* the flow, but, rather, to figure out how to *get into* the flow. Or, as Barry Stevens titled her book, *Don't Push the River* (it flows by itself). Stop fighting your life. Let go and let the river carry you to new adventures by the way you experience your life. In this way – and only in this way – it is impossible to lose.

Summary

STEPS TO SAYING YES

1. Create awareness that you can choose to say *yes* or *no*.
2. Nod your head – say *yes*.
3. Relax your body.
4. Adopt an attitude of "It's all happening perfectly. Let's see what good I can create from this situation."
5. Be patient with yourself. It takes times to adopt a "yes" approach to life. Say *yes* to you!

10

Choosing Love and Trust

Do you consider yourself a giving person? Think about it for a moment.

I asked this question of some of my students one morning, most of whom were married, and they all nodded their heads, meaning yes. Therefore, they were bewildered by their own reactions to the homework assignment I then gave them, which was simply, "Go home and say 'thank you' to your spouses." There was a distinct sense of discomfort in the room. You would have thought I had asked them to go home and beat their children! Finally, Lottie, who had been married for twenty-five years, piped up with, "Why should I say thank you to my husband? He should be glad I'm there!"

"Lottie, why *are* you there?" I asked. Her response was rather evasive – something to the effect that "he'd be a mess without me, and, besides, it would be too much trouble to leave." I repeated my question. After much prodding from me and the rest of the class, Lottie finally was able to acknowledge that her husband gave her a number of advantages: companionship, financial security and the feeling that she was not alone. I said, "Fine, so go home and thank him for that."

The following session brought the students into class with looks of dismay on their faces. They couldn't believe how difficult it had been to acknowledge the contribution of their spouses. Some were able to do the assignment, though with reluctance; others simply could not do it at all. Some reported that they also tried to thank their children and parents, and that, too, was very difficult. For the first time, they were forced to question just how giving they really were.

This did not mean that they were not contributing in other areas of their relationships. For the most part, they handled the details of the home, raised the children, and performed the obligatory tasks of the marriage. But were they really giving? Did they really know how to give? Or did they just exchange a "you do this for me" with an "I'll do this for you."

Needless to say, my students were quite dismayed by what they had discovered about themselves in this simple assignment. I assured them that most of us in our society do not really know how to give. Most of us operate on a hidden barter system. Few genuinely ever give anything away without expecting something in return – money, appreciation, love or whatever.

You might be saying, "What's wrong with getting back?" My answer is, "Nothing." However:

If all your "Giving" is about "Getting,"
think how fearful you will become.

More than likely the question will soon become, "Am I getting back *enough!*" This kind of thinking sets up an incredible need to control others so you won't feel shortchanged, destroys your peace of mind and creates anger and resentment.

Now you can see what's wrong with "getting" being the most important motivation for "giving." In fact:

Genuine giving is not only altruistic;
it also makes us feel better.

Why do we find it so difficult to give? My theory has two components. First, it requires a mature adult to give, and most of us have never really grown up. Second, giving is an acquired skill that few of us have mastered. These components are tied together and require a great deal of practice to achieve. The reason most of us have never practiced these skills is simple – it usually never occurs to us that we aren't behaving like adults or that we aren't giving. We unwittingly have deceived ourselves. And this is understandable. We *look* like we are adults and we *seem* to be giving people. What's going on underneath, however, belies appearances.

One of the most important lessons one has to learn in life is how to give, and *therein lies an answer to fear.* As babies we represent the ultimate of neediness. We come into this world as total takers. We have to take, or we will die. Our survival is tied up with the world nurturing us. We give little back. We don't care what time we wake our parents when we are hungry, or how loudly we scream and bother the neighbors when we want to be picked up.

Yes, parents often get a feeling of joy from the smile or the touch of their child and, in that sense, the child is a giver – but I doubt if the child spent the night pondering: "My life is abundant. I have so much to give away that I think I'll reward my parents with a great big smile tomorrow morning." No, their "gift" is on a rather primitive or reflexive level. In fact, a hungry belly in the morning will produce only loud shrieks of impatience.

As the years pass, we function as more and more independent beings, able to take care of ourselves – or so it appears. We dress ourselves, we feed ourselves, we earn a living. Yet there seems to be a part of us that never progresses much beyond the crib. Metaphorically, we remain frightened that no one will come to relieve our hunger – for food, money, love, praise and so on. Any relief in the way of "food" is only temporary; we know the hunger will come again.

Imagine what this dilemma sets up for us in the area of our daily living. We can't give. We can't love. We become, consciously or unconsciously, manipulative, because our survival is involved. We can't support the well-being of another person if their needs in any way conflict with ours. And how do we feel operating from the level of the playpen? Helpless, trapped, angry, frustrated, dissatisfied, unfulfilled, and, most of all, *fearful*.

What can be more frightening than depending on someone else for one's survival? As fearful adults, we ask the same questions we did as a child. Will they go away and not come back? Will they stop loving me? Will they take care of me? Will they get sick and die? As adults, we ask these questions about our mates, and often about our friends, bosses, parents, and even children.

People who fear can't genuinely give. They are imbued with a deep-seated sense of scarcity in the world, as if there wasn't enough to go around. Not enough love, not enough money, not enough praise, not enough attention – simply not enough. Usually fear in one area of our lives generalizes, and we become closed down and protective in many areas of our lives. Fearful people can be visualized as crouched and hugging themselves. Whereas this image represents the inner state of all frightened people, the outer manifestation can take on many forms:

Successful businessmen needing the boss's approval
Housewives who blame their husbands or children for the fact that they never lived their own lives
Independent career women who demand so much from their men that they are often alone
Men who can't tolerate their wives' independence
Company executives who make harmful, irresponsible decisions

They are all in some way operating out of a sense of fear for their own survival. They all are, in effect, crouched and withholding inside.

If you recognize yourself in this description, join the rest of us. There are few in our society who have actually been taught the secrets of growing up and giving. We have been taught the illusion of giving, but not the actuality of giving. As we have been taught to be careful in terms of our physical safety, we have also been taught not to let anyone con us or take advantage of us. As a result, unless we get something back, we feel used.

This is not to say that we can't enjoy what comes back to us, and paradoxically:

When we give from a place of love,
rather than from a place of expectation,
more usually comes back to us
than we could ever have imagined.

But if we are constantly expecting, we will spend a great deal of our lives disappointed that the world isn't treating us right.

I didn't find my way out of this painful state of existence until my mid-thirties, when it finally dawned on me that no matter how much I had in my life, *nothing would ever be enough!* The more I had, the more I wanted – more love, more money, more praise – more, more, more. Obviously, something I was or wasn't doing was keeping me from ever feeling satisfied. And, worse, it was keeping me in a state of constant fear that everything I had would ultimately disappear and there would be nothing left. I saw everything as the proverbial last drink of water in the desert, and I hung on for dear life.

It was time to try another way of being, since my old way was definitely not serving me, or anyone else in my life. As I described earlier, I sought out many teachers and got many answers. In essence, I learned that in order to get rid of the fear of lack, I had to do the *opposite* of what I had been doing up until that time. Instead of hanging on to everything for dear life, I had to start releasing, letting go, giving it away. If you think anything else in this book is difficult, wait until you try this one! It's really a Catch-22: It's easy to give when you feel abundantly endowed, but you only feel that way *when* you give, not before! So: FEEL THE FEAR . . . AND DO IT ANYWAY!

Again let me remind you that what I am presenting is a lifelong process that you can begin working on today. There is no magical potion as yet. It is amazing how long it takes to become a full-blown adult. In fact, one might consider it a lifelong task. I've been working on this for years and I'm still working on it. The good news, however, is that my sense of personal power and my ability to love and trust has increased at least 1,000% since I have been practicing giving it away. Many fears in the areas discussed below have completely disappeared for me. The rewards are monumental. I promise!

Give Away Thanks

Start by thinking about the people presently in your life and significant ones in your past. Put their names on a sheet of paper. Then list what each of them contributed to you in their own special way. Even if they brought you pain and you dislike them intensely, list their contribution to your life. As with Lottie, earlier, despite what she felt about her husband, there was much that he had provided her. Also, it's possible to make a gift even out of a negative.

I apologized to my son one day for the fact that at the time I got divorced I wasn't there for him emotionally when he might have needed me. I was too wrapped up in my own pain to help him with his. His answer was, "It's okay, Mom. That was the period of my life when I learned independence. That was a valuable lesson." He was able to thank me for my lack! In terms of mental health, he was far better off than if he had carried around resentment all those years. So, even if you perceive that someone has mistreated you, find the lesson you learned from them and put the contribution on your list.

Once you have listed all the gifts from various people in your life, systematically go about thanking them. If it is someone you haven't seen or heard from in a while, surprise them with a call or a letter simply acknowledging them for what they have contributed to your life. You will be amazed at the pleasure you will get – and give – from doing this.

With some people in your life, such as an ex-spouse, ex-friends or bosses, alienated parents or children, this can be especially difficult. To help rid yourself of present feelings of resentment and anger, try an exercise I learned in a workshop many moons ago:

Find an empty room and turn off the telephone. Put on some soothing music. Sit down in a comfortable chair and close your eyes. Visualize someone who brings up a lot of anger or pain in you. Picture them in front of you. First, surround them with rays of healing white light and tell them that you wish them all good things – everything they could possibly want in their lifetime. Thank them for whatever they have given you. Keep doing this until you feel your negative emotions leaving.

To say this is not easy is to utter the biggest understatement in the world. "Wish *her* good things? Are you out of your mind? I want to see her suffer for what she's done to me!"

The first time I did this exercise, I picked someone who had previously worked for me, and who had caused me a great deal of upset and pain. I had trusted him, and, to my mind, he had betrayed me. Note the victim mentality in full bloom! Obviously I was not taking responsibility for my experience of life at that time. As I went through the exercise, I experienced an incredible series of emotions.

First, I was shocked at the anger and resentment I was holding. I found it almost impossible, even in my mind's eye, to wish him anything good. My initial anger toward him was monumental. As I slowly released the anger, I got in touch with the pain I felt. This turned to anger at myself for allowing what had happened and for holding all my anger for so long. This turned into forgiveness of myself and of him. I was able to see both of us simply as people who had done the best we could at the time. I could then surround us both with healing white light.

This process took about an hour. When I began, I thought nothing much would happen. Wrong! I screamed, I cried, I hurt, I hated, I opened up, I forgave, I loved, I felt peace. I continued to do this exercise daily until I no longer felt anything negative about him and could freely wish him all good things.

I did this exercise for all the people in my life for whom I was holding any negativity, no matter how great or how slight. One of the people was my ex-husband. When I was able to reach the point in my visualization when I wished him only good, I phoned him and invited him to lunch. I simply said that there were some things I'd never told him and I wanted to do so now. He was pleased I called and we met for lunch.

I told him all the things that I really did appreciate about him when we were married and the qualities in him that I admire. My openness invited openness on his part, and he shared things about me that were loving as well. When I left lunch that day, I felt I had completed something that heretofore had been incomplete – and it felt wonderful.

If you cannot actually meet with people on your list, do it in your mind. Talk to them as if they were sitting in front of you and tell them what you want to say. Heal the relationship within yourself. In terms of your physical and mental health, it is just as good as if they were actually sitting before you.

We need to get rid of pain and anger before we can bring in love. When we hold negative feelings about people in our past, we carry those feelings to those in our present. Not only that, but we can make ourselves physically ill, as some of you may have already experienced. An excellent book to read on the subject of healing your body and mind is Louise Hay's *You Can Heal Your Life*. She has many exercises that will help you release the anger, pain and resentment that you may be carrying around with you.

So many people don't say thank you because they don't realize how important their thanks may be. Remember, *you count and your thanks count*. Don't let an opportunity go by to thank someone who has given you something – anything at all.

If this seems difficult for you right now, start with casual situations, such as saying to someone at work: "Thank you for that" or "I appreciate that" or "Thank you for being happy today; it's made me happy." *Thank you, thank you, thank you.* Start getting those words into your consciousness about everyone around you. Start thanking others instead of waiting for thanks to come to you. It is tough in the beginning, but it gets easier. Giving away thanks is like a muscle to be used. As we flex it, it gets stronger. It just takes exercise.

Give Away Information

So much of what we learn in life comes to us with great difficulty. And, for some reason, we have a tendency to want to see others struggle as much as we did. Turn this around and begin giving others as much help as you can possibly give them. Professionally, this can be very difficult. I can remember times when I felt threatened by those I felt were my "competition," and the tendency was to withhold information from them that would help them in their work.

Thank goodness, I felt the fear . . . and did it anyway. Some of the people I helped have become my good friends and part of my support system. Here, too, the giving has to be done with no expectations of return. More likely than not, however, the return will be enormous. One of my students asked what would have happened if one of them really had turned against me and used my information in a competitive way. My answer was, and is, that if I have enough belief in myself that I will "make it" no matter what anyone does, what is there to fear? It's a matter of developing trust in yourself and in your universe. For some reason, when you become a support to others you become bigger than you are. Moreover, when people use what they have learned from you, your effect in this world is greatly magnified.

Give Away Praise

For many of us, the people we find most difficult to praise are the ones closest to us – our mates, our children, our parents and sometimes our friends. A lot of the difficulty comes from anger and resentment. Yet, in some strange way, when we praise the people in our lives, we release the negativity and open the door for their being loving toward us.

Too many in relationships focus on the negative and have no difficulty reminding significant others of what they are doing wrong. It is no wonder so few relationships are going well. We want our loved ones to be affirming and supportive. It is important to surround ourselves with giving, loving and nurturing people. This implies the flip side of the coin:

You must become what you want to attract.
Be the kind of person you would want
to surround yourself with.

One of the doubting Thomases in my class asked me what happens if you give and give and give and get nothing back. I asked her for an example. She said that she gave and gave and gave to a man with whom she was trying to reestablish a relationship, and he refused to come back to her. I think she missed the point. In the first place, she was hardly giving with no expectations. She was expecting a lot! By her own admission, she felt that if she continued to give, he would see what he was missing and would finally come back to her.

I pointed out that it seemed more like a calculated con job, rather than an act of love. I suggested that she needed to release him and move on to someone who could better fill her needs. I reminded her that there is nothing wrong with the giving, but if our needs are not being met in a relationship, it is time to close that door, *with love,* and move on to someone else. Giving does not imply becoming a doormat. We are entitled to have our needs met. However, it doesn't serve us to be angry if a certain someone does not fulfill them.

Give Away Time

Time is something there never seems to be enough of, hence it is one of our most valuable commodities. It is also one of our most precious gifts. How do you give away time? You listen to a friend's problem, you write a note of thanks, you get involved in something bigger than yourself and become a participating member, you volunteer, you read a book to a child. All of these take you out of yourself and help you operate from a different part of your being – the part that is loving, nurturing and abundant.

David, one of my students, talked about one of his experiences of giving away his time. He volunteered for The Holiday Project that involved visiting hospitals at Christmastime. He described it as "an opening up" of his heart and taking it "out of the ordinary and petty into a different space . . . a high place." Notice what David was feeling from his contribution of time. He remembered singing to a child in a coma. The nurse had told him, "Sing to him . . . he'll hear you." He said it was beautiful and advised the rest of the class to open themselves up to such a contribution. "It's an incredible high!"

A dear friend of mine who recently had a stroke felt blessed and abundant at Thanksgivingtime. He volunteered, wheelchair and all, to help cook Thanksgiving dinner in a restaurant that was serving free meals to the homeless. He loved every moment of it. He knows he counts, even after his stroke.

Volunteering is also a wonderful way to spend holidays with your own children. One of my friends was aghast when her daughter, after opening fifty-two presents, said, "Is that all?" That was the last of that kind of Christmas for her daughter. Now, each year she and her daughter are part of the holiday project David talked about, and she has seen a transformation in her daughter. Instead of always wondering what she will be getting for Christmas, her daughter spends a lot of time creating things to take to the hospital and give away.

I want to say a word about volunteering in general. During my years at The Floating Hospital, I had many opportunities to observe volunteers. There were generally two categories: those who knew they counted and those who didn't. And what a difference there was between them!

The latter helped, not out of a sense of giving, but out of a sense of obligation: "I should be giving back to the community." Some of these used their volunteer experience as a way of proving to everyone else what "good" people they were. This is not to say that some were not of help. They were. Though some definitely were not! Their egos always got in the way. These were the ones who were not interested in what The Floating Hospital needed, but only in what would feed their egos. Hence, they often became more of a problem than a help to the staff. What was worse, they probably derived little sense of satisfaction or personal worth from their experience.

Those who knew they counted were a different breed entirely. They were there, silent but sure. They responded to our needs almost before we asked. They were diligent about being on time and never failed to show up when expected. They did anything required of them, no matter how menial it might have seemed. They did it with joy, knowing they were of use. They rarely talked about what they did – they just did it. And they were greatly loved for their contribution.

The difference between the way we operate in this world when we know we count and when we don't know we count is staggering. If you have not yet acknowledged that you count in this world, simply go around "acting as if" you do. Ask yourself, "If I really counted, what would I be doing in this situation? How would I be acting?" It really works.

So, knowing that you count, or "acting as if" you do, give away your time. What an incredible gift!

Give Away Money

Money is a huge confrontation for most of us. No matter how successful I become, I have moments when I see myself at the age of eighty-two standing on the corner with a cup in my hand, begging for money. I have found that many have this image of themselves. Where this comes from I haven't the foggiest notion. I have never really wanted for anything in my whole life. Yet the fear persists.

Fear about money often persists regardless of how wealthy we are. I recently read a newspaper account of an immensely rich man who still has nightmares about losing everything. For him, enough will never be enough. Years ago I heard a great line in a Grade B movie: "Security is not having money; it's knowing you can do without it." The fact that many of us have never been without money might be the problem. Here is another instance when a lack might have provided a very valuable lesson.

The answer to an obsession with money lies in loosening up and letting go. Within reason, begin to "give it away" with the belief that you will always find a way to have whatever you need. One friend of mine writes "thank you" on the checks with which she pays her bills. In this attitude, freedom lies – freedom to enjoy, to invest in yourself and others and to be a creative part of the flow. Giving away money can pay off enormously in actual dollars brought in, but, more importantly, in peace of mind. This is not to say that you should squander your money – balance is the key.

Give Away Love

As far as I am concerned, all of the "give aways" mentioned are about giving away love. But there are other ingredients in loving. For example, when we let someone be who they are without trying to change them, that is giving away love. When we trust that someone can handle his or her own life, and act accordingly, that is giving away love. When we let go and allow others to learn and grow without feeling our existence is threatened, that is giving away love. How many relationships do you know that look like that?

What often looks like love is not – it is need. As stated by Rollo May in *Man's Search For Himself,* "Love is generally confused with dependence; but in point of fact, you can love only in proportion to your capacity for independence."

TO LOVE IS TO BE ABLE TO GIVE.
AND NOW IS THE TIME TO BEGIN.

I've discussed giving away thanks, information, praise, time and, now, love. I'm sure you can think of other things to add to the list. You now understand that giving is about outflow. It is about letting go of your crouched, withholding self and standing tall with outstretched arms. When we really feel this sense of abundance, we truly understand the saying "My cup runneth over."

Giving from the position that "I count" enhances your ability to give. Like any other skill, however, it takes practice.

Whether you presently believe it or not, your life is already abundant. You simply haven't noticed it. Before you can accept abundance in your life, you have to notice it.

One way to increase your awareness is through what I call The Book of Abundance. Buy yourself a beautiful notebook. Start filling it by listing as many positive things in your life – past and present – as you can think of. Don't stop until you reach 150. Some of you will find more. When you feel you can't think of any more, you can. Just keep focusing on all the blessings in your life. No matter how small they seem, include them in your book.

Each day make entries in your book. Instead of a traditional diary – which for many is composed of doom and gloom, wish and want – create this book, which in effect simply states, "I have!" Note every positive thing, large or small, that happens – a compliment from a friend, a cheerful hello from the postman, a beautiful sky, a chance to contribute, a haircut, a new suit, nourishing food. *Notice* everything wonderful that happens to you.

Use reminders to keep you focused "on the doughnut, not the hole." Look for blessings, and you will notice them all over the place. They will envelop you. There is so much you are not seeing that is already there. There is no need to feel scarcity, when there is such abundance.

If you follow these directions, I suspect you will have a closet full of such books in a very short time. Refer to them often – especially when you are feeling a sense of lack. Lack is only in the mind. Some of the greatest givers I ever met were the poor I met at The Floating Hospital. I watched them and their sense of contribution to the people in their community, and it was joyous. Lack is not about money or things; it is about love. And love is always there for you to create when you are conscious that . . .

YOUR LIFE IS ABUNDANT, AND YOU COUNT!

In addition to your Book of Abundance, keep reading positive books, listening to motivational and inspirational audios and repeating your affirmations. Say to yourself, "I RELEASE MY FEAR OF LACK AND ACCEPT THE ABUNDANCE AND PROSPERITY OF THE UNIVERSE," and whenever you feel fear relative to money, or anything else for that matter, repeat this affirmation. It will give you peace. It will also remind you of the abundance that exists in your life at any given moment.

Keep remembering that you are aiming to get to the point where you are the giver. When you are aware of the fact that "you have," you can give. When you are a giver, you have nothing to fear. You are powerful and you are loving. The trick in life is not figuring out what you can get, but what you can give. There is so much power in this kind of thinking that it staggers the imagination.

Think about this: If you see that your purpose in life is to give, then it's almost impossible to be conned. If someone takes, they are simply fulfilling your life's purpose, and they deserve your thanks. When you act the giving adult, your fears are diminished . . . you realize you are meant to be used.

George Bernard Shaw summed it up beautifully in the quotation below. Reading these words daily will greatly help you to put things in perspective and give you the courage to move beyond your fear, so that you can be of great use to the world:

This is the true joy in life, the being used for a purpose recognized by yourself as a mighty one, the being a force of nature instead of a feverish selfish little clod of ailments and grievances complaining that the world will not devote itself to making me happy.

I am of the opinion that my life belongs to the whole community and, as long as I live, it is my privilege to do for it whatever I can. I want to be thoroughly used up when I die, for the harder I work the more I live.

I rejoice in life for its own sake. Life is no brief candle to me. It is a sort of splendid torch which I've got to hold up for the moment and I want to make it burn as brightly as possible before handing it on to future generations.

11

Filling the Inner Void

have talked about a lot of powerful tools: Affirmations, Saying Yes to Your Universe, Positive Thinking, Taking Responsibility, No-Lose Decisions, Choosing Love and Trust, Learning to Give and more. The reason these are powerful tools is that they open us to a place within, which, when tapped, allows us to feel "full-filled."

This place within has been given a multitude of names, some of which are: Higher Self, Inner Self, Superconscious, Higher Conscious, and God-self. I like the term "Higher Self," simply because it implies that we can move above that part of us that dwells on the petty things that cause fear, hate, scarcity and all other forms of negativity. It brings to mind a new plane of existence that has little to do with everyday upsets and struggle.

There is a body of psychologists who believe in the existence of the Higher Self and the influence it can exert upon the individual. Some refer to their work with the Higher Self as "Height Psychology." Others refer to it as "Transpersonal Psychology." There are also many educators and metaphysicians whose work encompasses the realm of the Higher Self.

They have proposed that this Higher Self is capable of a high degree of sensitivity and attunement to a harmonious flow within the universe. It is the container of many sublime virtues – creativity, intuition, trust, love, joy, inspiration, aspiration, caring, giving – everything we, in our heart of hearts, would like to experience.

Too many of us seem to be searching for something "out there" to make our lives complete. We feel alienated, lonely and empty. No matter what we do or have, we never feel full-filled. This feeling of emptiness or intense loneliness is our clue that we are off course, and that we need to correct our direction. Often we think that the correction lies in a new mate, house, car, job, or whatever. Not so.

I believe that what all of us are really searching for is this divine essence within ourselves. When we are far from our Higher Self, we feel what Roberto Assagioli has so aptly called "Divine Homesickness." When you are feeling this sense of being lost, or off-course, the thing to do to find your way home again is simply to use the tools that will align you with your Higher Self – and thus allow the good feelings to flow once again.

You might ask, "Where has this Higher Self been hiding all my life?" We often hear the expression "body, mind and spirit." It is used to define our whole being. Modern society has been primarily concerned with body and mind. The spirit part, which encompasses the Higher Self, has somehow gotten lost in the shuffle. As yet, there are relatively few places that teach anything about the Higher Self. So it is not surprising that we have focused almost totally on the intellectual and physical parts of ourselves. In fact, many of us haven't even been aware that we have a spiritual part.

Add to that the fact that many people don't even like the word "spiritual." They tune out the minute it is mentioned. The reason is that they confuse "spiritual" with religion and God. For those who are not religious, the word "spiritual" is a turnoff.

The way I use this word will be acceptable to you whether you are religious or not. When I speak of the spiritual, I speak of the Higher Self, the place within that is loving, kind, abundant, joyful, and all those other qualities I mentioned earlier. Believe me when I tell you that unless you consciously or unconsciously tap into that spiritual part within, you will experience perpetual discontent.

I am sure that every one of you has at times operated from the spiritual part of yourself without labeling it as that. Have you ever given something to someone and felt so good it brought tears to your eyes? Have you ever been so overwhelmed with the beauty of something, a sunset or a flower, that you were filled with a sense of abundance? Have you ever looked beyond someone's ugly behavior and felt only love for them as you saw their pain? Have you ever cried tears of joy in a movie when a character overcame a severe obstacle? If you did any of these things, it could be said you were operating from the Higher Self. You transcended the world of the petty – "She didn't even say thank you"; "He never picks up his dirty socks"; "Why doesn't he call?" – and touched a world of beauty beyond.

You experience an incredible high when your Personal Higher Self hooks into a Group Higher Self. If your heart swelled at the closing ceremonies of the Olympics – when you got a sense of how magnificent this world would be if we all acted as one for the good of all – you got a sense of the Group Higher Self. The power and love that can generate are phenomenal.

As you are undoubtedly aware, power, and even a sense of a high, can be generated by evil as well. The difference is the almost blissful feeling you get from all things generated by the Higher Self, which is inherently a loving space. Power from a negative place does not alleviate our Divine Homesickness. In fact, it takes us far, far from home. Thus, when the temporary sense of power leaves, you are left lost and lonely and frightened. When you operate from the

Higher Self, you feel centered and abundant – in fact, overflowing. When you experience this abundance, your fears automatically disappear.

The Higher Self is also in operation when you create "miracles" in your life – the power to lift a car if a loved one is trapped underneath or the power to accomplish a monumental task that everyone has told you is impossible. I have often heard people say, "I don't know how I did it, but I did!" Their power came from their Higher Self.

Now that I've introduced you to your Higher Self, let me show you an ultrasimple model of being. The model on the next page is not comprehensive; it leaves out many parts of our internal and external worlds. It does serve, however, to remind us that we can choose our experiences of life.

The Chatterbox, as you'll remember, is the part of us that tries to drive us crazy. It is the repository of all our negative input, from the time we were born to the present moment. It contains our childlike ego that needs constant attention and doesn't know how to give. The Conscious Mind sends orders to the Subconscious Mind based on the information it gets from either the Higher Self or the Chatterbox. We can train it to choose from either.

The Subconscious Mind is a storehouse of a huge amount of information. It also has access to the Universal Energy. It operates in a computerlike fashion, sorting out and finding information. For example, when you can't remember a name, and suddenly, when you are least expecting it, it pops up out of nowhere. Your Subconscious Mind has been at work. The Subconscious Mind takes its orders from the Conscious Mind. It does not question or judge. It does not know right from wrong or healthy from unhealthy. Remember the arm experiment in Chapter 5. When the Subconscious Mind was told, "I am a strong and worthy person," the arm was strengthened. When it was told, "I am a weak and unworthy person," the arm was easily pushed down. The Subconscious Mind believes what the Conscious

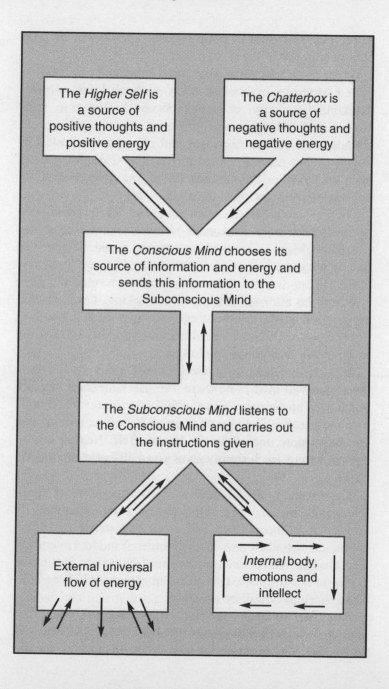

Mind tells it whether or not it is true, or even whether you believe it or not.

As the model suggests, your mind can choose to listen to your Chatterbox blabbering away with all kinds of self-defeating negativity, or it can choose to listen to your Higher Self, which is self-affirming, loving, giving and abundant. All of the exercises and concepts suggested in this book are geared toward having the Conscious Mind open its door to the abundance of the Higher Self as opposed to the scarcity of the chatterbox.

The Conscious Mind is often not aware that it is being run by the Chatterbox. And even if there is awareness, the Conscious Mind is so used to listening to the Chatterbox that, in the course of everyday events, it "forgets" to listen to the Higher Self and thus needs constant reminding. This is where the affirmations, positive thinking, tapes, books, sayings and whatever other tools you have come in handy – to remind your Conscious Mind that you do not have to listen to the Chatterbox any longer.

As with the Higher Self, the Chatterbox has always been there, and will always be there. No use lamenting the fact that it pops up every once in a while! I *guarantee* that it will. You must realize that you do have a Chatterbox within; and you have more, including the Higher Self. Neither one is right or wrong. Each simply gives you a different experience of life.

If you listen to the Chatterbox, your experience of life is fear-producing, and you stop yourself from expanding. If you listen to the Higher Self, your experience of life is joyful and abundant and devoid of fear. You, like everyone else, are an expert at listening to your Chatterbox. Your task is now to become an expert at listening to your Higher Self. Then true choice will be possible.

Why do so many positive things happen when the Conscious Mind chooses to operate from the Higher Self, and why does the reverse happen when it listens to the

Chatterbox? It seems that when the Subconscious Mind receives its orders from the Conscious Mind, it seeks to carry them out by connecting internally to the body, intellect and feelings. Thus, when it hears "I am a weak and unworthy person," it connects to your body and makes you physically weak. It connects to your feelings and makes you depressed and helpless. It connects to your intellect and makes you think stupidly. It also fills you with negative energy. When it hears "I am a strong and worthy person," it connects to your body and makes you strong. It connects to your feelings and makes you feel confident and alive. It connects to your intellect and makes you think clearly. It also fills you with positive energy.

What is more, outside yourself is a Universal Energy without which the world would not exist. In carrying out its orders, the energy of the Subconscious Mind connects to this Universal Energy, which manages to bring back exactly what you have "asked" for. If you put out "I am a weak and unworthy person," the universe obliges the Subconscious Mind and delivers all sorts of negative things. People step on you. You never achieve anything you want. Everything stands in your way, and you feel powerless to move anything aside.

When you put out "I am a strong and worthy person," the universe obliges the Subconscious Mind and delivers all sorts of positive things. People respect your strength and treat you fairly. You attain all sorts of wonderful things. Nothing stands in your way as you find the means to remove any obstacles. The key here is that just as your Subconscious Mind does not judge, neither does the Universal Energy.

Metaphysicians talk about Laws of Universal Energy. One of these is the Law of Attraction. You will recognize it as "like attracts like." When you send out negative energy, what will you attract? Negative energy. When you send out positive energy, what will you attract? Positive energy. Perhaps this makes clearer why it is imperative to train your mind to send out only positive thoughts.

Some of you might have trouble accepting the idea of Universal Energy. You don't need to believe this concept in order to tap into your Higher Self. However, when you can see yourself connected to something bigger than yourself, you no longer feel you must do it all alone. Your sense of power becomes highly magnified, and your fears are greatly diminished. This relates back to the Level 3 Fear: "I'm afraid I can't handle it." Now you can see that with the Universal Energy on your side, you can learn to trust not only yourself, but the universe as well. This kind of dual trust ultimately signals the end of fear.

One of the tools the Subconscious Mind uses to connect you with what you are looking for is your *intuition*. Those strange messages you get are the Subconscious Mind saying, "I found it!" Anyone who has experienced the power of intuition cannot deny that something is acting on our behalf if we listen to it. By learning to trust your intuition, "miracles" seem to happen.

Our intuition is always operating for us – usually, however, we don't act on it. When I made the conscious decision to start acting on thoughts that were coming through my head, amazing "coincidences" began to occur. My original "fear class" came about as a result of my intuition. At the time, I had a vague notion that one day in the future I wanted to teach a course on fear. I put it off indefinitely, largely because I was too busy with other things to write up the course description and outline and then find a school that would want me to teach such a course. It seemed like a lot of work.

One day, as I sat at my desk working, a strong message came to mind. It said, "Go to the New School." I couldn't figure out why this message came into my head. I never attended the New School for Social Research, I knew no one there. In fact, I didn't even know where it was. Out of curiosity, I decided to go. I told my secretary I was going to the New School, and she asked why. I said, "I don't know!" She looked at me strangely as I walked out the door.

I got into a taxi that delivered me right to the door of the New School. When I walked into the lobby, I asked myself, "What should I do now?" I saw a directory and looked at the various departments listed. My eye caught on Human Relations. "That's where I'm supposed to go." My mind reasoned that I was probably "sent" here to sign up for a great workshop they were offering. I was a workshop addict at the time. The idea of teaching at the New School didn't occur to me.

I found the door marked Human Relations Department and walked inside. No one was at the reception desk. I looked through the door on my right and saw a woman sitting at her desk. She called out, "Can I help you?" Intuitively, without "thinking" about it, I surprised myself by saying, "I'm here to teach a course about overcoming fear." Without my realizing it, I was talking to the head of the department, a wonderful woman named Ruth Van Doren. She looked at me with amazement and finally blurted out, "I can't believe that! I've been searching high and low for someone to teach a course about fear, and haven't been able to find anyone. And today is my deadline – all catalog descriptions must be in today."

She inquired about my credentials and was pleased with them. She then told me she had to run to catch a bus and asked me to quickly write up a course description with a course title. I did. She handed it to her secretary and ran out the door, thanking me profusely.

After she left, I stood in a state of shock. I had had no conscious intention of proposing a course that day. And what I had imagined would be an arduous task, taking months, took exactly twelve minutes! Ruth Van Doren wanted something, I wanted something, and the Universe put us together. How this works, I don't know. I simply know it works. The amazing thing is that had I consciously thought it through, I would never have approached the New School. I would have gone to Hunter College, where I went to undergraduate school, or to Columbia University, where I had obtained my advanced degrees. I knew a lot of people in both places. The New School would not have entered my rational mind.

It is worth noting that teaching that course was a turning point in my life. My experience was so positive and felt so "right" that I decided to leave my job of ten years to become an educator and writer. Oh, by the way, you might have guessed the course title I chose. It was "Feel the Fear and Do It Anyway"!

I'm sure you have heard of even more dramatic examples of the working of the intuition – lives being saved, people getting together despite tremendous odds, and other amazing happenings. The point is that we all have access to this intuitive power simply by starting to listen to the messages the Subconscious Mind is telling us. I suspect it works on instructions we have given it when we are clearly unaware we are doing so. We might have forgotten about it, but the subconscious never forgets. In fact, it works better when we take our Conscious Mind off the issue and let it do its work without our interference. That is why we get some of our most inspired ideas when we are relaxing or doing something other than the task that needs a solution.

Simply start paying attention to what you are being told and then act on it. If the mind says, "Call so and so," call them. If it says, "Go here," go here. If it says "Go there," go there. In the beginning you may be confused about whether it is your intuition operating or your Chatterbox or whatever. Just keep following the instructions, and soon you will be able to tell the difference. I'm at the point where I act on most of these seemingly "stray" thoughts that enter my mind, and I am amazed at the connections that have been made. In *Embracing Uncertainty* I devote an entire chapter to increasing the power of the intuitive part of who we are. Also entire books on developing the intuitive mind are available. It is an area definitely worth investigating.

I have begun to rely so much on my Subconscious Mind that when I am troubled by something, I simply say, "I ask my Subconscious Mind to find the solution for me." I then stop worrying and thinking about it. Somehow, easily and effortlessly, the solution comes. A particularly effective time to do this is as you go off to sleep at night. Simply let go and turn it over. You'll probably sleep much better as a result.

When you are upset, you are not letting in the abundance of the Higher Self. If you are aligned or "centered" as illustrated here, you feel yourself in a harmonious flow.

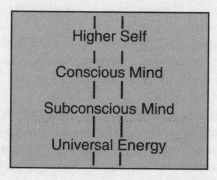

When you stay centered there is nothing to fear. You are tapping your source of power, and everything is okay. But how can you become centered, especially when you are upset?

If you are particularly rattled about something – let's say about getting a job you desperately want – the anxiety begins to build. You begin to feel that if that job isn't offered, your world will fall apart. The Chatterbox takes over and begins to drive you crazy, convincing you that it is the only job out there, and without it you will not survive. The Chatterbox is pulling you off center. It is then that you begin to use the techniques presented in this book.

You start to repeat your affirmations. You begin using your Pain-to-Power Vocabulary to put it in perspective. You put on beautiful calming music or a guided meditation or an affirmation audio. You begin to tap into your source of power – that place within where you can see the world as a safe and nourishing place. Keep remembering that it is just as realistic to think positively as negatively. And also remember the arm experiment. Positive self-talk works even if you don't believe it initially.

Say to yourself:

"This job is not my life. If I do not get it, it is because it is not for my highest good. If I am meant to have it, it will be mine. I can relax now and turn it over to my Subconscious Mind and the Universal Energy out there. All the answers I need are within me. It is all happening perfectly. There is nothing to fear."

While you are telling yourself these truths, work on relaxing your body. If you continue to feed yourself these affirming words long enough, you will eventually notice a warm calm come over your body and your mind and you will feel safe. Each positive statement pulls you, like a magnet, closer to the center . . . to your source. You've come to the place where all is safe. You've let go of the outcome, and there is nothing to fear.

It may take a while in the beginning to pull back to the center. So find yourself a quiet space and sit there for as long as it takes to make you feel better. Your calming background audio really helps get you to align faster. Not only does it set the mood and block out extraneous noise, but it also eventually conditions you to relax and feel your power the minute you turn it on.

What could you tell yourself if the problem is not your job, but your relationship?

"This woman [or man] is not my life. If we are meant to be together, we will be. If not, so be it. I trust that my Subconscious Mind and the Universal Energy are creating the perfect relationship for me. I can let go trusting that everything is happening perfectly. My life is full. My life is rich. There is nothing to fear."

Early in our marriage, my husband and I found a perfect house for us. It was more than we were prepared to pay; nevertheless, we put in a bid. I found myself beginning to be obsessed about having the house. The Chatterbox began:

"You'll never find the money for the down payment. If you sell your assets, you won't have anything to draw on. And what if you need money? If you lose that house, there will be no others out there as beautiful. But how are we ever going to raise the money?"

I quickly sat myself down and began the positive self-talk that would magnetize me back to the center.

"This house is not my life. If I am meant to have it, it will be mine, and the money will come to us easily and effortlessly. If it is not the house for us, we will find another one just as beautiful, perhaps more so. I'm turning it over to my Subconscious Mind to give me all the answers I need to know. It is all happening perfectly. There is nothing to fear."

All my obsessiveness stopped, and a warm calm came over me. Each time I felt myself listening to the Chatterbox, I returned to that place of safety and calm. The house was meant to be ours, because the money did come to us easily and effortlessly. By trusting the universe I could feel myself drawing toward me all that I needed to handle the purchase of the house comfortably.

I am convinced that

**IF WE DO NOT CONSCIOUSLY AND CONSISTENTLY FOCUS
ON THE SPIRITUAL PART OF OURSELVES,
WE WILL NEVER EXPERIENCE
THE KIND OF JOY, SATISFACTION,
SAFETY AND CONNECTEDNESS WE ARE ALL SEEKING.**

It takes practice. When people speak of "being on the path" or of life as a "journey," they are referring to the constant vigil required to train the Conscious Mind to listen to the lessons of the Higher Self, which, because of interference from the Chatterbox, elude us at times.

Let's go back and see how using your Whole Life Grid can provide the practice you need. I suggest that one of your permanent boxes be the Higher Self. Each day incorporate time to be quiet and to focus on the Higher Self, using the various tools suggested – affirmations, inspirational audios, meditation or whatever works for you. The best time to do this is in the morning, because it sets up the entire day. Focus on the Higher Self area of the grid before you go to bed as well – perhaps instructing your Higher Self to find the answer to some problem you may be encountering.

The Higher Self box is different from all the others because it is the one area of the grid that positively influences every other area of your life. It is from this higher place, above the petty, that you create value wherever you go and in whatever you do. Coming thus from a spiritual place, you enhance the quality of your relationship with the rest of the world – family, work, contribution, friends, personal growth, and so on. Keeping this in mind, your grid would look like the one shown on page 195.

The positive, loving energy that flows from a heightened spirituality will spill over into every area of your life. Those of you who have already discovered your spiritual selves understand what I am talking about. And for those of you who haven't, you have a real treat in store.

The Contribution box can serve to keep you aligned. When you become involved in a bigger energy motivated by the Group Higher Self, you are infused with power and purpose. It helps to contribute to something you believe in with all your heart. Make Contribution a permanent box in your grid as well. It will serve to remind you that you have so much to give, even if you don't think you do. Remember, "act as if" works whether you believe it or not.

WHOLE LIFE GRID WITH SPIRITUALITY

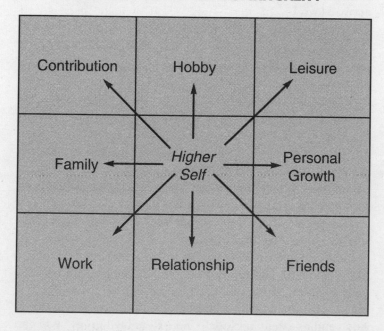

Contribution	Hobby	Leisure
Family	*Higher Self*	Personal Growth
Work	Relationship	Friends

It is not the purpose of this book to explain the world of the spiritual. What I hope to do, however, is whet your appetite, so you will be eager to learn more. I urge you to look at the laws of the universe as postulated by metaphysicians. I gave you only one; there are many others. Don't let the word "metaphysics" put you off. It simply means the study of that which is beyond the physical.

Metaphysical laws are amazingly simple to understand and can clear up many confusions about the way the world works. They can help you create a much greater trust in yourself and trust in the universe – which, of course, is the antidote to fear. These laws take a lifetime of practice, as does everything else in this book, but they will give you a sense of the direction in which you should be heading. For those of you who are religious and/or believe in God, you will see how these ideas can be incorporated in your beliefs. And, as I said earlier, if you don't believe in God, these laws apply as well.

I also encourage you to study the ideas of Roberto Assagioli, a great thinker in the area of transpersonal psychology. Assagioli is the founder of psychosynthesis, an amazing model for self-integration and self-realization. Psychosynthesis employs many techniques that are valuable in freeing us from past conditioning, resolving internal conflicts (such as, "I want to be taken care of" versus "I want to be totally independent") and awakening our loving and creative powers.

One of the powerful tools used by the practitioners of psychosynthesis and other disciplines is the *guided visualization.* This can be one of the most effective ways of quickly touching the Higher Self. There are a number of wonderful books written on the subject, and again I suggest you read them. But really to know the power of the guided visualization, you must experience one. Therefore, I encourage you to take a guided visualization workshop or buy audios that include one. Reading gives you an understanding, but going through one gives you the experience – a dramatic difference indeed.

In brief, a guided visualization requires that you close your eyes, relax your body and listen to the person giving you instructions. It uses the power of your imagination to see life as it would be seen if you listened only to your Higher Self. If you are fearful, your imagination is plugged into the Chatterbox, and often the only things you can conjure up are horror stories. With guided visualizations you can learn to push aside the Chatterbox for a moment and experience feelings and see mental pictures the likes of which you have never felt or seen before. The pictures are often of such beauty you will be moved to tears of joy. Even negative pictures that arise are valuable; they often reveal insights you have been hiding from yourself.

There are those who have difficulty creating visual pictures, and for them guided visualizations are not effective. If you are one of these people, don't worry: Simply use the other tools, such as affirmations, to help you find your way into the Higher Self. I do suggest, however, that you give visualizations a try.

It can be very effective to read aloud the visualizations given in books into your tape recorder, using as soothing a voice as you can project. By listening to visualization tapes by others, you will get a sense of the timing required between sentences to produce the full effect.

The following is a shortened version of a guided visualization I use in my classes and on my audio "The Art of Fearbusting."

Sit in a comfortable chair, with back straight, feet on the ground, hands comfortably on your lap. You have nothing to do but listen to my instructions and let whatever comes up for you come up. There is no right or wrong way to do a visualization. Just accept whatever comes up for you.

Now close your eyes . . . and keep them closed throughout the visualization. Take a deep breath . . . inhale all the loving energy in the universe . . . and exhale all your loving energy into the universe . . . Once more . . . in . . . and out . . . And once more . . . in . . . and . . . out. Feel how good it feels to begin to totally relax. Begin at the top of your head and work your way down to your feet . . . relax. Let go of the muscles . . . between your eyes . . . in your cheeks . . . mouth . . . neck . . . shoulders . . . back . . . arms . . . hands . . . chest . . . stomach . . . buttocks . . . legs . . . feet. . . .

Just totally let go . . . checking out any part of your body that may still be holding tension . . . and release it. . . .

Now I want you to think of a goal that you have in life . . . a specific goal . . . and you know that FEAR is keeping you from moving forward toward that goal . . .

Now what I'd like you to do is to imagine yourself approaching that goal "as if" you had no fear. . . .

I want you to see yourself approaching that goal with a sense of power and confidence in yourself . . . confidence that it will all be all right. . . .

What would you be doing . . . if you had no fear? . . .

See yourself. . . . What would you be doing next . . . if you had no fear? . . .

Look at the people around you. . . . How are you relating to them . . . with no fear? . . .

How are they relating to you? . . .

Just enjoy this sense of power and notice your ability to love . . . and contribute. . . .

And know that this is a feeling always within you . . . always a part of you. . . .

And it is within your capability to move forward in life with that power and with that confidence. . . .

See yourself . . . actualizing your goal . . . with your power . . . with your confidence . . . with your love . . . and with your contribution.

And slowly . . . start to bring yourself back to this room . . . knowing that that power is available to you . . . . As soon as you begin to act . . . the power will come forward.

Feel yourself in your chair . . . be present in this

room . . . listen to the sounds around you . . . and when you are ready, open your eyes . . . no need to rush. When you are ready, open your eyes.

Stretch and just feel the deliciousness of your power. It's all there for the taking.

I suggest you or a friend with a soothing voice speak this visualization into a tape recorder, leaving ample space between each instruction to allow your imagination to create detail and feeling in the various scenes.

For those in my classes who tune into visualizations, this one is very powerful. Many reported that for the first time they were able to see what the world looks like without fear. They reported that when they took away the fear, they were left with an abundance of love. They were startled by how beautiful the world appeared and how much they wanted to give to the people around them. If you have no concept of how the world can look without fear, it is hard to know what you are striving for. Once that vision is revealed to you, the Path is much easier to follow. You know when you are tuning in to the Higher Self and when you aren't.

Visualizations can also be used to find answers to questions about the meaning and purpose of your life, or to clarify your life goals, or to reveal important truths you hide from yourself. They have a multitude of applications and offer incredible insights – so much so that they are valuable tools used by educators and therapists.

I've presented you with a lot of ideas and a lot of tools, but to have them work effectively requires your trust. I've often been asked to prove that all I teach is true. I can only answer that certain things are not provable – at least, not yet.

I can't prove that a Higher Self exists. I can't prove that we are connected to a wonderful source of healing, nurturing energy. I can't prove that the Subconscious Mind can create "miracles" in both the inside and outside world. I can't prove that the tools I've given you work. But I do know that when I use these concepts as the model for my life, my experiences are transformed and I find myself absolutely in love with life and everything that it entails – all of it. I can't prove I am right . . . *nor can anyone prove I am wrong*. As Hugh Prather wrote in *There Is a Place Where You Are Not Alone:*

WHY CHOOSE TO BE RIGHT INSTEAD OF HAPPY
WHEN THERE IS NO WAY TO BE RIGHT?

Having experienced life from the vantage point of both the Chatterbox and the Higher Self, my choice is the latter. I will do whatever it takes to open myself up more and more to a mind and heart filled with love, joy, creativity, satisfaction and peace. That is my goal and, having used the techniques in this book, I have traveled many miles toward that goal. I look forward to the many more I intend to go. I trust we will meet along the way . . . if we haven't met already.

THE CHOICE IS MINE

WHEN I AM TUNED INTO MY CHATTERBOX	WHEN I AM TUNED INTO MY HIGHER SELF
I try to control	I trust
I don't notice my blessings	I appreciate
I need	I love
I am insensitive	I care
I am in turmoil	I am at peace
I am blocked	I am creative
I don't know I count	I count
I repel	I attract
I make a – difference	I make a + difference
I take	I give and receive
I am bored	I am involved
I am empty	I am filled up
I am filled with self-doubt	I am confident
I am dissatisfied	I am content
I have tunnel vision	I see big
I wait and wait	I live now
I am helpless	I am helpful
I never enjoy	I am joyful
I am always disappointed	I go with what is
I hold resentment	I forgive
I am tense	I am relaxed
I am a robot	I am alive
I am being passed by	I love getting older
I am weak	I am powerful
I am vulnerable	I am protected
I am off course	I am on the path
I try to control	I let go
I am poor	I have so much
I am lonely	I am connected
I am afraid	*I am excited*

12

There Is Plenty of Time

There you sit . . . filled with all sorts of information about how to make yourself powerful in the face of all your fears. What's next? What can I say to you to help keep you on course as you continue on the next part of your journey? First, the encouragement and motivation you have already received from this book will always be here for you whenever you need it. When you feel you are going off course or are being battered about by outside forces, come back and reread the parts that make you feel good.

Also, since *Feel the Fear and Do It Anyway* was originally published, I have written *Feel the Fear and Beyond to* give you practice using the exercises you have learned within this book. The more practice the better!

The biggest pitfall as you make your way through life is impatience. Remember that being impatient is simply a way of punishing yourself. It creates stress, dissatisfaction and fear. Whenever your Chatterbox is making you feel impatient, ask it, "What's the rush? It's all happening perfectly. Don't worry. When I am ready to move forward I will. In the meantime, I am taking it all in and I am learning."

When we wake up to the potential power within, our impulse is to grab it all "quick." The more we grab, the more it seems to elude us. There is no quick. There are quick – and wonderful – seminars, workshops, books, and audios that give you tools, but they are not quick tools. They are to be used and mastered throughout a lifetime.

I liken our impatience to an incident with my son when he was a little boy. I showed him how to plant a seed in a flowerpot and explained that soon, from the little seed, a beautiful flower would appear. I left him with his flowerpot and went on to do other things. Much later I returned to his room and saw he had placed a chair in front of the flowerpot and was sitting there watching it. I asked him what he was doing, and he said, "I'm waiting for the flower to appear." I realized I had neglected something in my explanation. So don't let me do the same thing to you.

So often when we are discouraged, thinking that we are learning nothing from all our efforts, changes are really taking place within us. We become aware of them long after they have been going on. Ultimately, my son did have his flower. One day he awoke and it was there. Although it didn't look like anything was happening, it was. And so it is with you.

One day, I threw a log on the smoldering embers of a dying fire and returned to the book I was reading. From time to time, I'd glance over at the fire and notice that there was no flame yet. There wasn't even the smoke that often signals a fire to come. Then, as I stared at the seemingly dead fire, flames suddenly burst out around the log. Patience means knowing it will happen . . . and giving it time to happen.

Again, it requires TRUST – trust that it is all happening perfectly. What do I mean by "perfectly"? I have come to believe there are only two kinds of experiences in life: those that stem from our Higher Self and those that have something to teach us. We recognize the first as pure joy and the latter as struggle. But they are both perfect. Each time we confront some intense difficulty, we know there is something we haven't learned yet, and the Universe is now giving us the opportunity to learn. If we go through the experience with this in mind, all the "victim" is taken out of the situation, and we allow ourselves to say YES. Thus, no matter what is happening at any particular time in your life, keep in mind that it is all perfect.

As long as you can remember that life is an ongoing process of learning, you won't have the disgruntling sense that you haven't made it yet. My experience of the last few years has shown me that so much of the joy in life is the challenge of figuring it all out. Nothing is as satisfying as those moments of breakthrough when you discover something about yourself and the Universe that adds another piece to the jigsaw puzzle. The joy of discovery is delicious. I know of no explorer who once having reached his or her goal has not wanted to go out and explore some more.

The challenge is to stay on the Path of the Higher Self. It is a far more enjoyable journey than the other paths you may choose to follow. You will know if you are on the right path by the way you feel. Trust your feelings. If the path you're on isn't providing you joy, satisfaction, creativity, love and caring, that's not it. Say to yourself, "Okay, I tried this, and this isn't it. What else can I try?" Don't be deceived into thinking that by changing the external, the internal will be changed. It works the other way around.

The path that needs changing is the one in your mind. This is not to say that once you become aligned with your Higher Self, you won't want to change things in your physical world, but it is your mind that has to be changed first – then all that is right will follow.

The Path is much like the experience of climbing a mountain. The climb is tough. But each time you stop to look around, the view becomes more spectacular. You see a greater expanse, and the "flaws" of the world below disappear as you see more and more of the whole. As you climb higher, you are detached from the heaviness below. You feel lighter. You feel freer. And you are propelled higher by the increasing beauty you see.

From this vantage point, you become more compassionate as well. You may dislike some individuals intensely for their cruel behavior. But from a higher place, you'll see more of the whole. These individuals are more than their "flawed" behavior. They, too, have a magnificent interior place, which they haven't discovered yet. Hence you'll begin to feel their sadness and not be so harsh in your judgment.

The journey upward is not always a steady climb. You may climb, then stop and rest, regroup. So, too, with the spiritual journey. Sometimes it may seem as though you have stopped growing. Not so. You are just consolidating your information.

Some of what you learn may require that you drop beliefs and behavior that have been part of you from the time you were born. Sometimes you'll experience an *aha!* and transformation will seem instant. Again, not so. Sudden insights are the result of all that has happened before. Your Subconscious Mind, like a computer, searches and sorts without your awareness and, when you least expect it, comes up with the answer. Insights happen more frequently, however, the farther along the journey you are. The Conscious Mind lets go of its resistance to new ways of thinking. It develops more trust. The initial stages are the most difficult and require the greatest concentration.

Sometimes when you think you've finally "got it," the Universe will step in to show you haven't. I've adopted a phrase of Lena Horne's that keeps me humble: "I've come a long way . . . maybe!" I have learned that there is always more to learn. And experience is our greatest teacher.

That is why I am so in love with the aging process. Youth so rarely understands what age allows us to know. We need to go through many life experiences before the power within is brought forward in all its glory. And as long as we see ourselves as unfolding beings, there is no wish to go back one single day – and age becomes a beautiful thing.

One of my favorite passages reflecting the agony and ecstasy of our journey is from *The Velveteen Rabbit* by Margery Williams. In the story, two nursery toys, the Skin Horse and the Rabbit, talk about becoming Real:

> "Does it hurt?" asked the Rabbit.
>
> "Sometimes," said the Skin Horse, for he was always truthful. "When you are Real, you don't mind being hurt."
>
> "Does it happen all at once, like being wound up," he asked, "or bit by bit?"
>
> "It doesn't happen all at once," said the Skin Horse. "You become. It takes a long time. That's why it doesn't often happen to people who break easily, or have sharp edges, or who have to be carefully kept. Generally, by the time you are Real, most of your hair has been loved off, and your eyes drop out and you get loose in the joints and very shabby. But these things don't matter at all, because once you are Real you can't be ugly, except to people who don't understand."

There is so much excitement and wonder in front of you. Sometimes you will experience the ecstasy of being in the flow. Sometimes you will experience the agony of being way off course. Remember you are not alone. This is a world filled with an abundance of support systems that are there for the taking whenever you are feeling troubled by life's experiences. One of my students said to me, "I read and read, and I assume one day one of those books is going to take!" I shot back, "No. *Nothing is going to take unless you take it!*" And so it is with this book and every source available to you. DON'T WAIT FOR IT TO TAKE! TAKE IT! Use it. Live it. Absorb it. Unless you use the muscle that lifts you to your Higher Self, it will weaken – just as your body weakens when it is not used. If you think you need additional help, then by all means, enlist the aid of a professional. Take action. Nothing is going to work for you unless you do the work.

Say YES to life. Participate. Move. Act. Write. Read. Sign up. Take a stand. Or do whatever it takes for you. Get involved in the process. As Rollo May wrote in *Man's Search for Himself:* "Every organism has one and only one central need in life, to fulfill its own potentialities." He goes on to say that joy is the result of using our powers to their fullest, and for that reason, joy, not happiness, is the goal of life.

And what is joy? It is something that expresses the ebullience of the spiritual part of ourselves. Joy is characterized by lightness, humor, laughter and gaiety. Lighten up. If you have ever been around a person who is centered and enlightened, you are struck with their humor and ability to laugh at themselves. All the brittleness is gone and only fluidity remains.

I took time as I was in the middle of writing this chapter to join in the Hands Across America event.* As we all stood singing "Hands Across America," the theme song, I looked at the faces around me. For those few moments in time, everyone participating *knew* they made a difference. It was reflected on their faces. They were joyous. They were loving. They were caring. They were touching the highest part of themselves. Many were crying tears of joy. It feels so good to align yourself with some higher purpose. *To become involved is to reduce our fear.* We become bigger, we move away from that "feverish, selfish little clod of ailments and grievances complaining that the world will not

---

*On May 25, 1986, more than five million people paid 10 dollars to join hands, all at the same time, and form a line that stretched 4,152 miles from New York to California . . . all to raise money for the hungry and homeless and to call attention to America's poor. It was called Hands Across America.

devote itself to making [us] happy." We move into true adult status, where we have much to give to this world.

So commit! Commit yourself to pushing through the fear and becoming more than you are at the present moment. The you that could be is absolutely colossal. You don't need to change what you are doing – simply commit to learning how to bring to whatever you do in life the loving and powerful energy of your Higher Self. Whether you are a bank teller, housewife, corporate executive, student, street cleaner, teacher, film producer, salesman, lawyer, or whatever, it's yours to give. As you live this way, moment by moment, day by day, in perfect time, you will find yourself moving closer and closer to Home. The paradox is that when you stay close to Home, you can go anywhere and do anything without fear. The Divine Homesickness disappears as you find the place where we all are connected as loving human beings. Whatever it takes to get you there, **FEEL THE FEAR AND DO IT ANYWAY!**

Bibliography

Most of the following books and audios were in my head and heart when this book was published in 1987. I've included a few more recent resources which I thought you would find useful. Enjoy!

Assagioli, Roberto, *Psychosynthesis*. New York: Penguin, 1976

Bolen, Jean Shinoda, *The Tao of Psychology: Synchronicity and the Self*. San Francisco: HarperSanFrancisco (1982) 2005.

Canfield, Jack, *The Success Principles™: How to Get from Where You Are to Where You Want to Be*. New York, HarperCollins Books; 2005.

Chopra, Deepak, *The Spontaneous Fulfillment of Desire: Harnessing the Infinite Power of Coincidence*. New York: Harmony, 2003.

Cousins, Norman, *Anatomy of an Illness*. London: WW Norton & Co Ltd, (1997) 2005.

Dobson, Terry, and Miller, Victor, *Giving in to Get Your Way*. New York: Delacorte Press, 1978.

Emery, Stewart, *Actualizations*. Garden City, NY: Dolphin Books, Doubleday and Company, 1977, 1978.

Ferguson, Marilyn, *The Aquarian Conspiracy: Personal and Social Transformation in the 1980s*. Los Angeles: J. P. Tarcher, 1980.

Ferrucci, Piero, *What We May Be: The Visions and Techniques of Psychosynthesis*. Los Angeles: Tarcher Publishing, (1982) 2004.

Fields, Rick, with Peggy Taylor, Rex Weyler, and Rick Ingrasci, *Chop Wood, Carry Water: A Guide to Finding Spiritual Fulfillment in Everyday Life*. Los Angeles: Jeremy P. Tarcher, 1984.

The Foundation for Inner Peace, *A Course in Miracles*. London: Arkana, (1975) 1997.

Frankl, Viktor, *Man's Search for Meaning*. London: Rider Books, (1959) 2004.

Gawain, Shakti, *Creative Visualization*. London: New World Library, (1978) 2002.

—, *Living in the Light: A Guide to Personal and Planetary Transformation*. Mill Valley, CA 94941: Whatever Publishing, 1986.

Hay, Louise, *You Can Heal Your Life*. London: Hay House, (1984) 2002.

Hill, Napoleon, and Stone, W. Clement, *Success Through a Positive Mental Attitude*. New York: Pocket Books, 1960.

Holden, Robert, *Shift Happens!: Powerful Ways to Transform Your Life*. London: Hodder & Stoughton, 2000.

Jampolsky, Gerald, *Love Is Letting Go of Fear*. Millbrae CA: Celestial Arts, 1979.

Jeffers, Susan, *Embracing Uncertainty: Achieving Peace of*

Mind As We Face the Unknown. London: Hodder & Stoughton, 2002.

— *End the Struggle and Dance with Life: How to Build Yourself Up When the World Gets You Down.* London: Hodder & Stoughton, 1996.

— *Feel the Fear . . . And Beyond, Dynamic Techniques for Doing it Anyway.* London: Rider Books, 1998.

— *Feel the Fear and Do It Anyway.* London: Hodder Headline Audiobooks, 2005. (3 hour CD)

— *I Can Handle It!: 50 Confidence-Building Stories to Empower Your Child.* London: Vermilion, 2002.

— *Life is Huge!: Laughing, Loving, and Learning From It All.* London: Hodder & Stoughton, 2005.

— *Opening Our Hearts to Men: Taking Charge of Our Lives and Creating a Love that Works.* London: Judy Piatkus Publishers, Ltd., 1989.

— *The Art of Fearbusting.* London: Hodder Headline Audiobooks, 1986. (1 hour CD – a live talk)

— *The Fear-Less Series: Inner Talk for a Confident Day . . . Inner Talk for a Love that Works . . . Inner Talk for Peace of Mind,* London: Hodder & Stoughton, 1992.

— *The Feel the Fear Guide to Lasting Love.* London: Vermilion, 2005.

— *The Little Book of Confidence.* London: Rider Books, 1999.

— *The Little Book of Peace.* London: Hodder & Stoughton, 2001.

Kanin, Garson, *It Takes a Long Time to Become Young.* New York: Doubleday and Company, 1978.

Keyes, Ken, *Handbook to Higher Consciousness*. Marina Del Rey, CA 90291: Living Love Publications, P.O. Box 550, 1980.

—, *How to Enjoy Your Life in Spite of It All*. Marina Del Rey, CA90291: Living Love Publications, Distributed by DeVorss and Co., P.O. Box 550,1980.

Kushner, Harold, *When All You've Ever Wanted Isn't Enough: The Search for a Life That Matters*. New York: Summit Books, Simon & Schuster, 1986.

Levine, Stephen, *A Gradual Awakening*. London: Rider and Company, 3 Fitzroy Square, nd.

May, Rollo, *Man's Search for Himself*. New York: Delta Publishing, 1953.

Murphy, Joseph, *The Power of Your Subconscious Mind*. New York: Bantam Books, 1963,1982.

Paul, *Life Is a Spiritual Experience: Metaphysics Made Practical*. Girdwood, AK 99587: Flower of Truth Publishing Co., P.O. Box 763, nd.

Peale, Norman Vincent, *You Can If You Think You Can*. London: Heinemann, (1974) 1991.

Peck, M. Scott, *The Road Less Travelled: A New Psychology of Love, Traditional Values and Spiritual Growth*. London: Rider Books, (1985) 2003.

Porter, Eleanor H., *Pollyanna*. New York: Farrar, Straus & Giroux, 1912.

Prather, Hugh, *There Is a Place Where You Are Not Alone*. New York: Doubleday Company, 1980.

Probstein, Bobbie, *Return to Center: The Flowering of Self-Trust*. Marina Del Rey, CA 90294: DeVorss & Co., P.O. Box 550, 1985.

Rann, Michael and Elizabeth Rann Arrott, *Shortcut to a Miracle: How to Change Your Consciousness and Transform Your Life*. Jeffers Press: P.O. Box 5338, Santa Monica, CA 90409, 2006.

Rossman, Martin, M.D. *Healing Yourself: A Step-By-Step Program for Better Health Through Imagery*. New York: Walker and Company, 720 Fifth Avenue, 1987.

Sheehy, Gail, *Passages*. New York: Bantam Books, 1976.

—, *Pathfinders*. New York: William Morrow and Co., 1981.

Sher, Barbara, and Gottlieb, Annie, *Wishcraft*. New York: The Viking Press, 1979.

Small, Jacquelyn, *Transformers: The Therapists of the Future*. Marina Del Rey, CA 90294: DeVorss and Company, 1982.

Williams, Margery, *The Velveteen Rabbit*. London: Egmont Books Ltd, 2005.

Williamson, Marianne, *The Gift of Change: Spiritual Guidance for Living Your Best Life*. San Francisco: HarperSanFrancisco, 2006.

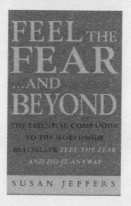